THE TIMES.
2.2.83

**The A1 Locomotive**
Project No 60163 TORNADO

Let's make an A1!

bition, which opens on Friday at the London Toy and Model Museum, Craven Hill, Paddington, London. The exhibition will last for seven months.
The toys shown are (left to right):

Porsche 356A Coupé, 1958, second casting; Kodak delivery van, 1935; and Shredded Wheat delivery van, 1934, second casting. The last Dinkies were made in Britain in 1979. (Photograph: Suresh Karadia).

SHREDDED WHEAT

Live Steam Scale Model L.M.S. Mogul Gauge 0 (7m/m)
BASSETT-LOWKE (RLYS) LIMITED
59 Cadogan Street, London, SW.3. England

acetrains

L M S

# Brilliantly Old Fashioned

## New Cavendish Books

London

# Brilliantly Old-Fashioned

## THE STORY OF ACE 0 GAUGE TRAINS

### ALLEN LEVY

ACE Trains & New Cavendish Books

Published by New Cavendish Books in association with ACE Trains – 2005

British Library Cataloguing-in Publication Data.
A catalogue record for this book is available from the British Library.
ISBN: 1–904562–07–8
Edited by Juliette Levy
Production Consultant Narisa Chakra
Designed by Mike Ennis

Photography – ACE archive – Peter Viccari – Mike Ennis and John Agnew.
The author thanks the HRCA for permission to reproduce certain articles from their Journal and also
N J Groombridge whose photograph was used on the front cover.

New Cavendish Books, 3 Denbigh Road London W11 2SJ.
T: 0207 229 6765 E: sales@newcavendishbooks.co.uk

Authors Note – Much of the material used in this book has been reproduced from unique working documents correspondence, e-mail attachments etc. Whereas in a few cases the quality of reproduction may be impaired I felt that in the interests of authenticity this was an appropriate trade off.

Printed and Bound in Thailand

*DEDICATION*

**To all those (many hopefully mentioned in the text) who encouraged us to turn back the clock and rewind it.**

CONTENTS

Preface                                                              9

Foreword by John H Kitchen                                          11

Introduction                                                         12

1995-1996:   Taiwan to India – E/1s and E/2s.                       20

1996-2000:   Madras Interlude – C/1s, C2s and EMU's                 62

2000......:   Bangkok, Widening Horizons – 'A4s and all that'       72

Footnote on Collecting                                             125

Table of Manufactured Items                                        126

ACE Box identification                                             130

A4 Names                                                           132

Index                                                              133

# ACE TRAINS
LONDON

*Catalogue No.1*
*1998*

## Bassett-Lowke Railways

## A Century of Model Trains

Allen Levy

The Institute of Chartered Accountants in
England and Wales.
(Incorporated by Royal Charter, 11th May, 1880.)

——

EXAMINATION CERTIFICATE.

——

This is to Certify that

Allen Lawrence Levy

passed the FINAL EXAMINATION to the satisfaction of the
EXAMINATION COMMITTEE on the 24th, 25th, 26th and
27th November, 1959.

GIVEN under our hands this 3rd day of February, 1960.

Member
of the
Council.

Secretary.

*Toys at*
## THE LONDON TOY & MODEL MUSEUM

The London Toy & Model Museum
21-23 Craven Hill, London W2 3EN. 01-262 7905/9450

POST CARD

*AU REVOIR*

Dear

*Allen Levy and Narisa Chakra cordially invite you to celebrate*

*their seven years at the London Toy & Model Museum*

*and to wish the museum*

*continued success under its new management.*

*Buffet, Music and Steam locomotives.*
*at*
*The London Toy & Model Museum*

7pm - midnight                    Black Tie

RSVP By April 30th : Golden Age, 3 Denbigh Road, London W11 2SJ 01- 229 6765

The London Toy & Model Museum
21/23 Craven Hill, London W2 3EN

# ACE TRAINS
LONDON

*Coach Supplement No.1*
*1999*

# PREFACE

## Bringing it all back . . .

This is the story of an unlikely revival. Popular gauge 0 tinplate in three rail ready-to-run – available at most good toy shops – had prematurely run into the buffers due to the outbreak of the Second World War. It staggered on in the post-war years much diminished, with a variety of clockwork offerings by Hornby and (lower down the toy train chain) Mettoy, Chad Valley as well as a few other rather obscure firms. By complete contrast, Bassett-Lowke offered a fine range of gauge 0 material in the 1950s, which for the first time made absolutely no pretence at catering for the sub adult market. It would be fair to say that this company had throughout its long and distinguished history rarely sought out this market with any conviction.

By the 1960s Bassett-Lowke had effectively stopped production at a time when the management (following the death of Roland Fuller) had virtually no understanding of that side of the gauge 0 business in the UK. However, an active market in used gauge 0 equipment was growing, inflated by demand from the Continent. An abortive attempt to revive Bassett-Lowke in the late 1960s saw a few offerings but nothing approaching volume production.

In 1995 ACE Trains came along to light the fuse that would lead to the rebirth of traditional three–rail gauge 0 trains. Several years ago we were joined in the market place by Corgi's efforts, via the skills of Len Mills, to breathe life into the dormant Bassett-Lowke name they had bought some years earlier, and which incidentally I had declined to revive again when offered it in the 1990s.

The ensuing story charts the progress of this project and although there has been an significant investment in time and money, ACE has proved that with determination, strange and wonderful things are possible. Sentimentally, gauge 0 tinplate-style trains never really went away but had just reposed in the surviving products of a bygone age. ACE changed all that.

**ALLEN LEVY**
**London 2005**

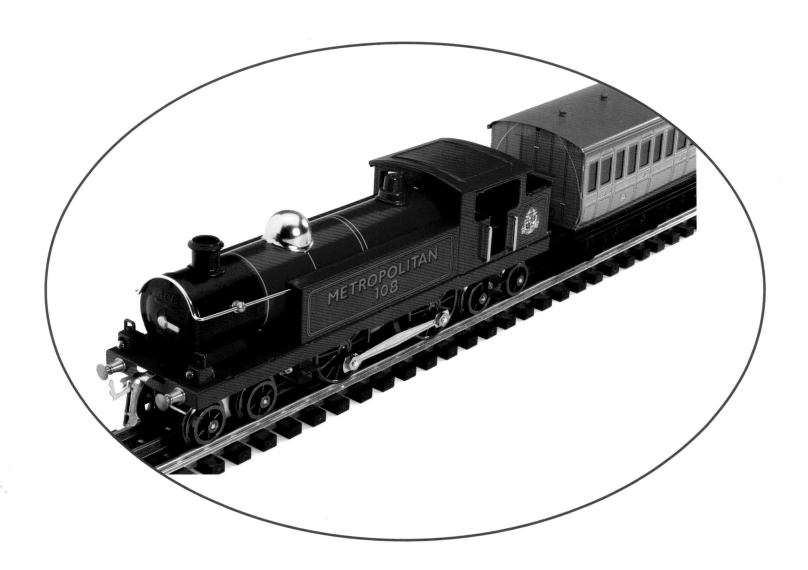

# FOREWORD

I have known Allen Levy for at least 40 years but even so I am not altogether sure why the distinguished author of this volume invited me to provide the foreword in the first instance. Perhaps it is my lifelong interest of railways in particular, engineering in general and aeronautical development, all fostered by that incomparable publicity organ of Meccano Ltd, the 'Meccano Magazine'. Consequently I have been, since a very tender age, a passionate admirer and collector of the 'products of Binns Road', especially of Hornby series – British and guaranteed and to a lesser extent Hornby Dublo. Tin and diecast trains are in my blood therefore.

It was not by accident that ACE Trains decided to follow the traditions and high quality production of Hornby tinplate locomotives, initially with its version of the aesthetically pleasing Hornby No. 2 4-4-4 tank engine. The classic outline did not follow any particular locomotive, but as with all things engineering – both full size and model – if it looks right almost invariably it is. The new E/1 ACE locomotive incorporated a very efficient and robust electric mechanism, a refinement the original never aspired to, and this fact coupled with very high quality materials, workmanship and finish (even the brass dome was gold plated) ensured its immediate success, aided by rakes of bogie coaches to suit most regional tastes.

The company has found a niche market and thereby filled a gaping hole left by the great toy and model 0 gauge train manufacturers of the past. This initial promise is still being fulfilled and even exceeded by current production ten years on. Allen Levy has for decades been deeply involved with model railways – who can forget his superb 'A Century of Model Trains' and subsequently his magnum opus as editor of The Hornby Companion Series, eight books over 15 years devoted to the products, publications and history of one company, Meccano Ltd, surely a feat never attempted before and doubtless will never be equalled. Both works were published by New Cavendish Books, created by Allen Levy in the early 1970s. These then are the solid foundations on which ACE Trains is built, right at the cutting edge of the resurgence of 0 gauge popularity. Could this marque join the illustrious names of the past; Bassett-Lowke, Marklin et al? All the signs are there, the next ten years promise to be very exciting indeed.

**John H. Kitchen**
**President, The Hornby Railway Collectors Association**

# INTRODUCTION

## 10 YEARS OF ACE TRAINS

I debated whether to write the ten year history of ACE Trains in the first person or whether to hand it over to one of the many excellent contemporary model railway historians, several of whom I had published in my New Cavendish Books days.

I always thought it a pity that Frank Hornby never published any personal memoirs concerning his company's products in the manner of W.J. Bassett-Lowke, his upmarket rival. Was he very involved with the design choice of product or merely in strategic and financial matters? His later career as an MP must have restricted his activities at Binns Road on a day-to-day basis at the very least. I find it odd that we know more about the lives of many lesser figures from that period than we do about an inventive and entrepreneurial genius of the stature of Frank Hornby. I decided to write this work in progress in the first person.

Not only did many of the great toy and model train makers not tell their stories but also very few *verbatim* anecdotes remain to colour in the personalities. As I am open to questioning and *ad hoc* conversations at various meetings throughout the year, this aspect is less of a problem in the case of ACE. I am often told by those who have read *The Bassett-Lowke Story* which I edited and co-published in my New Cavendish Books days, that Dudley Dimmock's recollection of life in the various Bassett-Lowke shops gave a unique insight into the philosophy and methods of the company. Dudley's story chronicled the more human side of the company's endeavours, rather than the lusted after catalogue images which masked a multitude of decisions, good or bad. In the 1960s, I rescued the Bassett-Lowke Minute Books (ranging from 1909 through to the 1950s) from being thrown out during a clear-out of the archive at Northampton. They are now on long term loan to the Bassett-Lowke Society. I find it extraordinary that barely one decision as to why this or that model was made, or what quantity, is revealed – the inclusion of which would be gold dust for collectors today.

So returning to this modest work, while I cannot boast that all human life is revealed, an amusing anecdote might get the ball rolling. I would briefly comment on the title I have chosen for this book (previously used as a heading in a series of ACE ads.) 'Brilliantly Old Fashioned'. This phrase links a superlative with a pejorative in the sense that 'old fashioned' does not sit well in the pantheon of cool today – nor do model trains and its connotation of pasty looking men in sheds or lofts, and their long suffering wives.

This links very directly to a recent incident in which a rather grand lady neighbour harangued me for writing too many letters concerning the over planting in the communal gardens we abut. She concluded her rant by saying I should get myself 'a proper job' and then would have less time to write letters to her. I retorted that my job gave more pleasure to countless men than she could possibly imagine. To this day, she probably thinks I operate in the sex business in some form or other. I deliberately did not colour in the nature of my work now or in the past. It would have been all too difficult, given that virtually every family in my neighbourhood (including my verbal assailant) seems to be linked to law, insurance or investment banking. I doubt if many would have seen the sanity of following my particular career pattern. Thinking outside the box is one thing, ACE Trains and all that preceded it quite another.

As with so many things in my life, ACE Trains was not planned. It was not something I was moving inexorably towards. Neither, for that matter, were my earlier incarnations; first as a chartered accountant (professional practice, followed by a little City 'whizz kiddery' including a spell as a director of The Falkland Island Company) then as joint-founder of Bassett-Lowke Railways in the late 1960s, moving on in the 1970s to writing and publishing *A Century of Model Trains*, through my company New Cavendish Books. This led me on to further publishing with New Cavendish in partnership with Narisa Chakrabongse, great granddaughter of King Chulalongkorn (who was immortalised on stage and screen by the actor Yul Brynner in 'The King and I'). I mention this not only as an exotic connection but also because Thailand would figure significantly in the later story of ACE. How wheels turn in life. In 1980, Narisa and I founded The London Toy and Model Museum, which we ran until 1989, when personal issues led to the sale of the entire undertaking.

Then in the 1990s came ACE. The notion of ACE Trains was sparked by a chance meeting with Andries Grabowsky (of award winning HO manufacturers Holland Rail) at a supper hosted by one of my oldest model railway confreres Marcel Darphin (founder of Darstaed which is famous for gauge 0 finescale and reproduction 40cm Marklin – style tinplate coaches). Of course, the meeting took place close to the town of 'Zug' (train) in North East Switzerland – where else!

Marston's Hosiery Factory, John Street  C 1930.
Then and now from a small hosiery factory to ACE Works.

**1** Ivan Scott, founder of Steam Age, with a finely modelled stationary under-type engine of the early 20th century

**2** Allen Levy, driving force behind Bassett-Lowke (Railways), with the first of his definitive series of model locomotives. Patrick Stirling's famous Single No 1. Each model will be individually numbered

# Model makers extraordinary

*Some of the finest commercially-available models are supplied by two British companies—Steam Age and Bassett-Lowke (Railways). David Fisher recalls their history and achievements*

Chelsea. On London's Thames-side. Home of artists and writers. Of fashion makers. A centre for antiquities. And now, for model steam locomotives.

In a corner shop, along Cadogan Street, Chelsea, are the headquarters of Steam Age and Bassett-Lowke (Railways), two companies associated in this business of model railways. The location of the shop is not so paradoxical as it may seem, for the models that come from the shop have for their *cognoscenti* the same sort of aesthetic appeal that works of art have for others. But with this difference: the model locomotives work and thus have an appeal to the engineer that is in many men.

The two companies, though sharing common premises and having a common purpose to encourage and satisfy the interest in model railways, had different beginnings, have rather different though overlapping areas of activity, are independent, and are the chosen pursuit of two very different men.

Bassett-Lowke (Railways) is the re-creation of a famous name, possibly the best-known and most reputable name in model making. It is now run by a young man, Allen Levy, **2**, chartered accountant by profession, a model-locomotive collector of long-standing, and now proprietor of the company almost by accident, though one suspects that little is allowed to happen by accident in this precise man's life.

Steam Age, by contrast, is altogether a new company, founded in November 1965. It will therefore be celebrating its fourth birthday during the *Flying Scotsman* tour. Founder of the company is Ivan Scott, **1**, film maker and producer by career, who has been interested in steam and models all his life, especially 'anything that would haul you around'. Perhaps his film-making has given him a special approach to the amalgamation of illusion and realism that is so much a part of model making. His interest is in the big models, from ½ in to ft scale (2½ in, 64 mm, rail gauge) up to 1½ in scale (7¼ in, 184 mm gauge). Levy's prime interest lies in the smaller fellows, particularly 0 gauge (1¼ in gauge), the smallest size that can be realistically fired, but also up to ½ in scale. Both put a premium on perfection.

This present story cannot be told without relating that of the old Bassett-Lowke company. The founder was the late W J Bassett-Lowke who was originally an engineering apprentice in his father's business of boiler-making and general engineering, J T Lowke and Sons of Northampton. 'Bassett' was his mother's maiden name and her family too, were boiler-makers, Bassett and Sons. So young Wenman, for such was his Christian name, came from good 19th century engineering stock.

He was always, even before his apprenticeship, a keen and able model maker. But in the year 1900 (when he was working with Crompton Ltd, the electrical engineers of Chelmsford) he went to the international toy exhibition in Paris. He was instantly impressed by the model locomotives he saw there, especially those from Germany, which possessed a scale appearance the like of which was quite unknown in the United Kingdom. He returned to England determined to found a model engineering business, which he did, along with young friends who also worked in his father's firm.

Initially, Bassett-Lowke bought his models from abroad, particularly Germany. His first mass-produced model was the LNWR *Black Prince* to 2½ in gauge, and this was the first commercial attempt anywhere to produce a model locomotive that had a close and realistic resemblance to the real thing. Bassett-Lowke had started a new industry: the 'tin plate' railway model.

Interest in model railways grew at a phenomenal rate and by 1914 the hobby was thoroughly established, with both indoor and outdoor sets, and right up to the passenger-carrying trains built for large estates. Many types were available ranging from 0 gauge (1¼ in) up to quarter scale, 3 in to the foot, 15 in gauge. In the smaller models, methylated spirits was the favourite fuel, though the bigger engines were

*Reproduced from the magazine 'Engineering' dated September 1969 edited by Kyle Bosworth. I met Kyle on the 1969 Flying Scotsman Tour of the USA. Over 30 years later Leonard Woods, an ACE enthusiast, told me that a neighbour of his in a small village nestled in the Sussex Downs knew me. Such are the wheels of coincidence.*

*The proposed live steam ex Barry Port Tank in American guise. This was the last gauge 0 project proposed by Bassett-Lowke for Bassett-Lowke Railways in 1969. Projected tooling costs of over £20,000 reflect how far out of commercial touch the old company was in 1969. The project went no further than this sample whose whereabouts today remains a mystery.*

*In the absence of new production I busied my self with dealing in used items.*
*Those were the days when an ad in the Sunday Times would yield Marklin 'Kings' and 'Jubilees' and endless gauge 0 Hornby.*

3 Allen Levy is also initiating another new Bassett-Lowke series, in 1/72 scale. Appropriately, the first in the series will be the *Flying Scotsman*, shortly to be followed by the *Royal Scot*. True miniatures, and each a collector's piece, the models will be exquisitely accurate in detail and available in a presentation jewel-type box

coal-fired. Clock-work units had been produced, but also with the faithful external appearance that was to characterize Bassett-Lowke's work. Railway models were not their only product however. They had already produced a range of stationary engines and Bassett-Lowke had, from his earliest days, a keen interest in ship models which, in later years, materialized in those magnificent models, sometimes just shells, sometimes cutaways, that graced the premises of the shipping lines.

In the locomotive field, by 1914, model making was in some respects ahead of railway practice. The first ½-scale Pacific (4-6-2), the *Colossus*, in fact had no prototype! It was built about 1912 for Captain J E P Howey to designs of Henry Greenly who then worked for Bassett-Lowke. The 'model' had a style that was perhaps ten years in advance of the railway companies. Howey and Greenly were later to be associated in the founding of the 15 in gauge Romney, Hythe and Dymchurch Railway, Kent, which still operates with ever-increasing success during the summer months.

As a business, Bassett-Lowke had a number of distinguishing features. They were, for example, one of the first—if not the first—mail-order firm. Bassett-Lowke never sold through normal retail outlets. They had their own shop at the works in Northampton and in 1908 had opened their own premises in Holborn in London. Later, they opened other shops in Manchester and Glasgow, but a great deal of their business continued to be done through the post.

Many famous model makers worked for Bassett-Lowke and, individually and collectively, they built a reputation that has never been bettered in the model-making industry. Indeed, their reputation stood on the same plane as Rolls-Royce. Like Rolls-Royce, too,

their products were never for the mass market: they were aimed strictly for the well-to-do, monied, middle classes.

Many of the very early models are now collector's pieces and change hands at high prices in the auction rooms of Christies' and occasionally Sotheby's.

Throughout the 1920s, the business continued to expand so that they were making sales almost everywhere throughout the industrialized world. The number of types produced multiplied and they began to carry the long list of accessories that were available to enhance the realism of model layouts. They also produced the kits of parts for the enthusiast to do his own assembly and finishing. They were also building large numbers of architectural and industrial models, such as power stations, dock installations and the like. But, whatever the model, the accuracy of the reproduction of detail, in form and colour, always characterized the Bassett-Lowke product.

The 1939-45 war also circumscribed the company's activities but amongst their contributions to the war effort were a large number of 'recognition' models—ships, tanks and aircraft—for the armed services, to enable friend to be distinguished from foe. This was an activity that had also been practised in the 1914-18 war and carried on, though less strenuously, between the wars.

After the 1939-45 war, the firm at first seemed to revive but during the early 1950s they never really adapted to changing conditions, though they continued to maintain those standards on which their reputation had been based. The founder, however, was becoming an old man—he was about 80 when he died in the early 1960s—and railways—particularly steam locomotives—were beginning to suffer their eclipse and it was not yet time for the revival of interest in steam that began, perhaps, four or five years ago.

After the death of W J Bassett-Lowke, others took over and finally the original company divided into two: at Northampton where they put the emphasis on making industrial models and Allen Levy's new company of Bassett-Lowke (Railways), operating from the premises in Chelsea. There exists a friendly association between the two now independent Bassett-Lowke companies, with the Northampton works continuing to do work for the Chelsea branch, particularly in the repair of old models.

Both Steam Age and Bassett-Lowke (Railways) are thriving concerns, exporting over 70% of their outputs. They claim that they are the only makers producing practical 0 gauge steamers, and recent successes include selling in the Japanese market, no mean achievement this, where only the highest possible standards have any chance of forcing an entry. Japan has her own very fine model-making industry which, at the moment, fulfils much of the United States demand.

The market for railway models in the US is very large: one estimate puts the figure at $66 M a year, covering everything from H0 (Half-0, ⅛ in gauge) up to 15 in. Between the wars, Bassett-Lowke enjoyed a great reputation in the Americas and the new companies are now out to obtain their shares of that market—one reason they are on the *Flying Scotsman* export train.

The US market, like Japan, demands the highest standards of model-making. The very nature of the American economy and the American approach to life makes it impossible for them to produce the models to the standards they demand. Fortunately, however, they can afford to buy from those who still have the skills and inclinations to strive for the perfection of detail that the model railway connoisseur seeks.

As in the past, much of the standard

**4** The *Virginia*, 7¼ in gauge, which is being delivered to her Houston owner aboard the *Flying Scotsman* exhibition train. Built by Steam Age, she is a faithful replica of a New York and Hudson River 4-4-0 wood-burning locomotive and tender of the last century. The model is complete with lights, bells and cow-catcher and is finished in a livery of blue, red and black

achieved by Bassett-Lowke and Steam Age models stems from the fact that they start work from the original, full-scale drawings and they use castings only where castings are called for and fabricate where required. Even with the most modern die-casting techniques it is not possible to fool the connoisseur where fabrication should be used. To use Allen Levy's words, 'We fabricate right down to the whistles'—and that for 0 gauge models!

Levy and Scott have an American associate, Henry Goldsmith, who is looking after their marketing activities. It is his opinion that this attention to detail is an essentially British—he says 'English'—trait. Nowhere else, he says, can you find the situation where the maker hangs on to the model until it satisfies him, never mind that the buyer is willing to take it.

Nowadays, in addition to manufacture at Northampton, Levy is calling on two 'units', general engineering works, that do the basic manufacture for him. The models then go the rounds for completion. One man may be the specialist at cab fitting—no single pressing for these models—and the enthusiast is the first to know if the inside of the cab is not right. The livery, too, is another feature that must be right; the colours have to be true, and so does the 'lining', and in these days there are few craftsmen around prepared to do this sort of work, and have the knowledge to do it. This is not a new feature of British model-making: Bassett-Lowke also had his 'sub-contractors' and fine old characters some of them were. The arrangements, both then and now, have many of the features of the pre-industrial revolution 'cottage industries', and certainly do not

fit easily into modern commercial/industrial accounting.

Many of the famous types in British steam locomotives are available from Cadogan Street, following through the old Bassett-Lowke series. A good example is the 0 gauge reproduction of Sir William Stanier's 2-6-0 Mogul, originally introduced in 1937. The new 1968 series of Moguls, 18 in long and weighing 3 lb 8 oz, have brass boilers tested to 45 lb/in² and fired with a vapourizing spirit lamp; the piston valve cylinders are of hard brass and the piston rods of brass; the piston valves, stainless steel. The valve gear is Greenly Walschaerts, reversing from the cab. The engine exhausts to the chimney. Each engine is individually numbered, and they are finished in LMS black or red, enamelled and lined. Cost: £90, say $220.

Levy's own series is to be the Classic Gauge 1 series (1¾ in track). Each production series will be made in a limited batch and individually numbered. When the batch is sold, no more will be made. Initially, the series will comprise four classic pre-grouping engines (engines made before the railway in Britain were grouped into the four regional companies in 1923). The first three of the series will be Patrick Stirling's 8 ft Single No 1, followed by the Wainwright 'D' and the Great Western *City of Truro*. Levy's idea is to produce a definitive series showing the development of the steam locomotive, rather than random examples of the art. The specification of the models is superb. The UK cost will be £200.

Another new range will be real miniatures: 1/72 scale. First in the series will be *Flying Scotsman*, **3**. Again, in limited numbers, and beautifully

presented in a jewel-box. The next in this series will be the *Royal Scot*.

Scott's show-piece on the exhibition train is the *Virginia*, **4**. The model has already been sold to a Houston buyer whose condition of purchase was that it would be delivered aboard the *Flying Scotsman* exhibition train. It is a 4-4-0 New York and Hudson River locomotive and tender to 7¼ in gauge. It is the first commercial model of Buchanan's famous 19th century wood-burner, and took two years to build from design to steam trials. It is powerful, fast and decorative, reviving the pioneer spirit in which the original was built: complete with lights, bells and cow catcher, and painted gloriously in blue, red and black.

Much of Steam Age's range comprises famous names in British locomotives, but there are also a number of fine stationary engines and traction engines of earlier days, a ¾ in scale model of a Bristol tramcar, and an exhibition model of the tug *Conservator*, complete with every conceivable detail and driven by a two-cylinder marine steam engine. Details of these and many more models of the Steam Age and Bassett-Lowke lines are described in a new presentation catalogue that the companies have prepared, which also includes facsimiles of earlier Bassett-Lowke catalogues.

But although these other, non-railway models are available, it is in the steam locomotive that interest is concentrated. With the virtual disappearance of the steam locomotive from the railways, there is an immense resurgence of emotional interest in steam that seems certain to establish the model steam locomotive as part of the permanent antiquarian scene.  □

*An early E/1 alongside a Van Rymsdyk 4-4-4 of 1950s vintage. John's original company made a wonderful series of controlled clockwork locos and some trams. The locos were sold in spherical containers. These two locos pictured on the lunch table at the Van Rymsdyk's Mill in the South of France where they retired after John departed from his post at The Science Museum.*

After much to-ing and fro-ing concerning an existing project of Andries'– to reproduce the erstwhile clockwork Hornby 4-4-4 Tank locomotive in electric – a deal to underwrite the manufacture of over 1000 of these locomotives in over a dozen liveries was sealed. In fact, the decisive handshake was made on our little family boat 'Volta' bobbing about in St Mawes Bay, off Southern Cornwall's Roseland Peninsula. ACE Trains was formed in 1995 and initially traded as Alchem Trains Ltd. We could not obtain name ACE Trains Ltd at that time as it was already in use by an air conditioning company. As they say in New York – go figure!

This reproduction of one of Hornby's elegant tank locomotive designs gave rise to the now famous ACE E/1. So by 1996 British-style tinplate was once again available in the UK, although it would take our French friends a little time to realise that a worthy successor to AS Trains of France had been born. The story of that company's line must surely lurk as a work in progress in somebody's PC, although that is another story.

So why did I once again return to manufacturing tinplate-style toy and model trains? Well, a cousin of mine – a big cheese in the advertising business – recently e-mailed me after receiving an ACE newsletter by mistake and commented: 'Allen, I always thought you were so cool, but you're really an *anorak*'. I suppose to those slick ad men, studying railways in all its forms does not compare with the superficiality of staring at pickled sharks. So I must confess my time spent train spotting does qualify me as a latter day *anorak* even though I did not possess one in those far off days spent on wet platforms at King's Cross Station – N2s to the left A1s, A3s and A4s to the right, the noise, the smell…..

It would not be telling the whole truth about my time at Kings Cross if I did not mention the agonising that I endured when hovering around WH Smiths news stand on platform 1. Could I pluck up courage to buy *Health and Efficiency* or at the last moment switch to *The Railway Magazine* as a female assistant loomed into view. From my long association with the international world of model railways sex has never been far from trains. Today I still have to live down the picture of myself on page 93 of my book *A Century of Model Trains*.

While on the subject on advertising people, I will digress. When we ran The London Toy and Model Museum, I placed a small ad in The Sunday Times pointing out that ours was 'a great café with a wonderful museum attached'. Several years later, in the best ad world tradition, a well known agency coined the far more famous line:

'An ace café with a great museum attached' referring to the

V & A Museum. I will never know whether this was inspired by our earlier ad, but it was prescient as in 2005 we are opening an ACE Museum, in the Leicester area, with a great working layout attached – touché.

Referring back to the *anorak* observation, what is it that keeps such a disparate and, in the main, entirely likeable group of men – and in several notable cases, women – locked into the world of model and toy trains, or for that matter the broad spectrum of general toy collecting? Well, apart from the obvious nostalgic allure and the Proustian search for times gone by, it may simply be that, in the case of model railways (and let's use that term in the generic sense encompassing toy and model forms), nothing took its place as a domestic hobby for the steam and latterly diesel generation. Even real rail travel has enjoyed a renaissance – news of its demise was far too premature, as indeed was similar news of its three-rail gauge 0 equivalent.

Perhaps recollecting a mere ten year history of ACE seems premature, but it should be remembered that the prolific pre-war output of Hornby gauge 0 lasted just 19 years, and even Bassett-Lowke's main period of large scale production only lasted some ten years prior to World War II. Before 1930 virtually everything was made by, or based on the production of, Bing or Carette in Germany. As will be mentioned later, Bassett-Lowke's post-war production endured for about 15 years, with most of that being small run production which ACE could not contemplate in its programme today. In a short while, the overall production of ACE from its various factories will far exceed the output of its Bassett-Lowke post war equivalent. Post-war, Hornby gauge 0 tinplate excelled in quantity only with their four wheeled clockwork locomotive carriage and wagon stock. However, this was the last gasp of the Hornby toy shop market which would await the plastic offerings of 'Thomas the Tank Engine', as well as the red ex-Great Western engines that were woven into the Harry Potter stories decades later.

It took Hornby some time and financial pain to realise that the world had moved on and Hornby boys had grown up. It was the realisation that playing with model trains was principally an adult pursuit that led to the resurgence of Hornby Trains (nee Tri-ang). This, coupled with the eventual move of production to China, enabled Hornby to satisfy the more exacting standards of the adult market and thus save the day.

## Setting the Scene - 1990s

Gauge 0 ready-to-run is now in new territory so a little background might be useful.

In the Darwinian sense ACE was an anachronism in 1995, a little like Morgan Cars but with the important distinction that those 1930s *manqué* gems from Malvern were not absent from the market for over four decades.

Large scale production of gauge 0 effectively ended in 1939. Bassett-Lowke's ability to farm out small scale lines of models in the post-war years, mainly to the model builder Vic Hunt, relied on the fact that a small but relatively wealthy clientele existed in those product starved years of the 1950s. Admittedly, a range of tin printed locomotives, both freelance and, in the case of the 4P and A3, excellent representations of the real thing were available (all these based on pre-war tooling). This however was no longer popular toy shop business. Following the demise of Bassett-Lowke in Northampton in the early 1960s ready-to-run, factory-made gauge 0 ceased in the UK. Odd pockets of what I will describe as kitchen table and garden shed production sprung up and Bassett-Lowke Railways (see *The Bassett-Lowke Story*, New Cavendish Books) were reduced to putting triangular stickers on one-off models made by a variety of people. I am often asked by new collectors whether this or that is genuine Bassett-Lowke. Broadly speaking, the last batch of steam moguls made in Northampton and put out by Bassett-Lowke Railways, Cadogan Street in 1969 denotes the end of genuine Bassett-Lowke production. The Bassett-Lowke label fixed to any model after 1969 has no connection with Northampton and in collecting terms must be considered as one-offs. Present day Corgi/Bassett–Lowke, however, is a genuine attempt to resurrect the original line.

Later in 1973, Lima of Italy plunged into the gauge 0 two-rail market with a series of plastic two rail electric steam, diesel and electric style locomotives, as well as rolling stock. Curiously they ignored the fact that in the UK, 1/43 was the accepted scale and not 1/48 and 1/45 as applied in the USA and the Continent. Too much product was made and I suspect that over 30 years later some unsold material still exists. However, three-rail equipment was available in the 1970s through the surviving products of Hornby and Bassett-Lowke, but had become extremely expensive. A very active and extensive cottage industry of spare parts grew up to support the restoration and running of these old warriors. this was, of course, linked to the ever growing societies and associations dedicated to the preservation and study of firms such as Hornby and BassettLowke and in the case of the TCS many others. So, many gauge 0 vintage trains kept rolling but many more were left on shelves by their owners.

It became accepted wisdom that new batch produced metal three-rail gauge 0 was a vanished dream. Had I not met Andries Grabowsky in Zug I think that wisdom would have prevailed. Sometimes a stab in the dark can reveal more than any market research – risky but true. Ten years on, we have no doubt that ACE has revealed a very real demand for all those trains whose conception was cut short by World War II; the rumoured Hornby A3, inevitably an A4 (let us not consider Bassett-Lowke's 25 guinea offerings of the 1938 equivalent) and possibly a Castle – surely a must. Furthermore, there was a latent demand for tinplate coaches that would resemble the real thing as distinct from the rather ersatz offerings of Bassett-Lowke, post-Carette and Hornby. Edward Exley produced excellent gauge 0 coaches throughout the pre-war and post-war period under review, but these cannot be considered to be in the tinplate tradition as they veered more towards the scale market, albeit not by today's demanding scale standards.

Well, ACE has and will deliver all these things, namely the left over programmes of its predecessors. It is a supreme irony that, together with Len Mills efforts during his days with Corgi, the early part of the 21st century has become the new 'golden age' of three-rail British outline gauge 0. All I can say is that the wartime generation deserves to have its dreams brought to reality, as indeed do the younger enthusiasts hitherto not exposed to the glory of gauge 0, who may have decided to move on from the prolific post-war output of 00. ACE will never rival the large manufacturers, apart from the pure glamour factor and, in many instances, the superior performance of their output. Metal tinplate-style trains will always look, feel and sound superior to those made of plastic – it's just a hard fact of life, or perhaps my purely unequivocal point of view.

I will not engage in a long discourse on the finescale kit market in gauge 0 which has burgeoned since the 1960s. I should say that a real distinction should be drawn between playing trains, with all the fantasy it entails, and on the other hand, an attempt to reproduce real pieces 'dot for dot' (borrowing a printing term) at a scale of 7mm to 1ft. The late and very great Stanley Beeson was an extremely good friend who often amused me when he lamented how few 'Hebrews' were attracted to the hobby (I usually agreed with him but said I hoped to some extent I was redressing the balance). He went on to tell me that to reproduce the cab of an LMS 4P he would have to make the cab roof the thickness of a cigarette paper. So each to his own, but as a manufacturer it is an enormous relief not to be governed by these harsh parameters. ACE will always strive to create the spirit of the original, but not to the last nut, bolt and rivet.

Finally this is a story about people involved in a venture they passionately believe in. In my own case I have been encouraged by my dear wife Charlotte – often puzzled – but always totally supportive of this unique little company and its worldwide and seemingly around the clock activities.

*The spin round St Mawes when Andries and I decided to seal our other voyage in ACE Trains.*

# CHAPTER ONE – 1995-1996: TAIWAN TO INDIA, E/1s AND E/2s

## PREPARATION FOR THE ACE AGE

Let me begin by defining some terms while at the same time attempting to describe the aims of the ACE Trains project. ACE was initially described by the finescale brigade as tin toy train makers. This brings me to the description of the generic term, 'tinplate'. I believe this phrase was first coined by Louis Hertz in his wonderful book 'Riding the Tinplate Rails'. The word tinplate was never meant to only describe the material used in many early toy trains but rather to indicate the coarse and even impressionistic style of the equipment put out by firms such as Lionel, Ives, Bing, Marklin, Carette and later on, Hornby and, to a lesser extent, Bassett-Lowke. These evolving toy trains possessed an element of fantasy and as the years went by many more scale elements were drawn in. Witness the 1939 Lionel Hudson (hardly a scrap of tinplate in it) and Marklin's wonderful locomotives of the 1930s. Hornby and Bassett-Lowke were also heading in that direction and indeed the latter's late pre-war and post-war production was almost a crossover point to the world of realistic model railway equipment.

ACE arrived some time after all these marques had ceased making gauge 0 equipment in the tinplate style. Both the American and German markets had, by the 1970s, an established trade in the manufacture of replicas of many classic 1930s locomotives and rolling stock of Lionel and Marklin in standard gauge and gauge 0.

Preceding this, in the late 1960s, was the extraordinary production of Wilag, in association with the late Count Giansanti's Fulgurex Company. This production included replica gauge 1, 56cm Marklin CIWL and PLM cars, an amazingly daring venture which unfortunately ended in financial tears. Reproduction tinplate for the gauge 1 market never really caught on and even the Fulgurex reproduction of the extremely rare Marklin Rheinuferbahn in gauge 1 was a very slow seller. In what I call the Van Gogh effect, everyone wants one now. The same phenomenon is beginning to become prevalent with obsolete ACE lines. As a footnote to this observation, Wilag was the true precursor to Aster of Japan, as well as all the later Chinese gauge 1 live steam makers who followed.

Britain, like France, was slow to realise the potential of this revival movement – replicas that looked liked the originals but operated without all their foibles. Of course, another feature of this 'movement' was the ability to play trains with the reproductions while preserving mint examples of the originals for purely collecting purposes. This was surely influenced by the massive rise in values of the classic toy trains of the 1930s. Nowhere was this more felt than in the relative prices of Marklin originals and their many latter day clones.

In the 1980s a French based partnership, AS, produced a line of extremely evocative locomotives and rolling stock which, while not copying the style of Jep, Hornby et al, were very French in their own unique tinplate style. Complex screening techniques were employed for passenger cars, while locomotives were sprayed. Although some of the motors used were not so successful, towards the end of production in the early 1990s some extremely potent motive power emerged. The AS Metro and Est Inter Urban sets are particularly sought after and the whole of the AS range has become a collecting sub-culture notwithstanding its relative newness.

However the true inspiration for the revival of three-rail coarse scale model trains was Elettren of Italy in the early post-war years. Their coach production has never been surpassed in this field and their magnificent FS Pacific (despite a tendency for some of its castings to warp over time) was the inspiration for our own A4 (E/5) Pacific over fifty years later. Both, I suggest, are landmarks in post war gauge 0 ready-to-run motive power.

## HOW IT ALL BEGAN . . .

Pre ACE Trains, Andries Grabowsky was introduced to Ron Budd, who was the UK agent/importer of the Darstaed range of 40cm Marklin coach replicas. There followed some discussion about developing a project to make a small run of reproduction Hornby locomotives in vintage tinplate style. Ron Budd suggested an electric version of a 1920s clockwork 4-4-4 tank locomotive. Apart from some rare examples for the French market no electric version existed. They decided to make around 300 examples in SR green and black, the rarest original Hornby types. During the development of the tooling it became apparent that the manufacturer required a much larger order, with a commitment to underwrite the considerable tooling costs. The tool required for bending and rolling steel was expensive and this, together with blanking tools for cutting flat metal, cabs, tanks and so on, skyrocketed the bill up to a high five figure sum.

It was a major undertaking from the outset, given that a relatively simple locomotive such as the E/1 required over 100 parts from a variety of specialist sub-contractors. For example, the gears had to be (and still are) cut on a 1930s Japanese machine operated by its original Japanese owner living in Taiwan. The project should be seen in the context of being the first factory produced reproduction of a British outline vintage locomotive, namely the Hornby 4-4-4 tank whose original production ended in the late 1920s. An original clockwork Hornby model had been sent to Taiwan in 1994 as an example of what was required, before ACE Trains was up and running, therefore parts such as wheels had already been cast. That is why clockwork pattern wheels were fitted to the E/1 rather than the slightly more elegant wheels of the contemporary Hornby electric locomotives. It was at this stage that I took this project over as a principal, rather than as a distributing agent.

To our relief, when the E/1 went into service from 1996 onwards they became universally acclaimed as one of the most rugged, dependable and powerful four coupled electric locomotives in the history of three-rail gauge 0 – apart from an occasional clunk over certain types of track! These locomotives were made almost entirely in Taiwan, a costly yet highly competent base from which to manufacture a relatively short run – by Far Eastern production norms - of around 1300 pieces.

Our first major catalogue issued in 1998 showed the full range of E/1s and flagged up our much under-produced E/2 range – more of which later.

Unlike vintage Hornby, the first batch of E/1s were not fitted with bearings. This was typical of ACE Trains' contrarian view that confounded the 'If it ain't broke don't fix it' dictum by improving on what customers were already satisfied with – very worthy but heavy on the bottom line. So, midway through the production run the factory started fitting phosphor bronze bearings to the driven axles. All E/1s were fitted with the somewhat temperamental Uhlenbroch AC/DC box. Originally intended for HO, it proved quite reliable, except that people trying to engage the AC mode were invariably using pre war controllers. Thus getting between 12 and 16 volts through the box while the loco was stationary proved to be rather hit and miss. This was chiefly due to the fact that the output on these controllers was difficult to regulate within such narrow limits. A few E/1s were issued as DC versions, only because a dedicated DC user had no need of this rather complex AC/DC device.

The red boxes these locomotives were issued in were a way of paying homage to their illustrious Hornby predecessors. The first two to be issued were in Southern Green livery and were named 'John

Kitchen' and 'John Beadsmore', the former being the long serving Chairman (now President) of the The Hornby Railway Collectors Association, the latter its journal editor. Many of the commercially available examples were also named according to customer requirements (see illustration). An audacious aspect of this project was to produce five French versions of the E/1, some of which followed the Anglo-French practice of the 1920s – British outline body, foreign lettering. It was audacious because nobody had reproduced a French Hornby- style locomotive before (ignoring the earlier AS efforts as they were not true Hornby reproductions) and selling anything to the French is, putting it mildly, problematic. For many years this proved to be true, then *voila!* Just when stocks of the French E/1 were virtually exhausted - thanks to a good uptake by British enthusiasts - there was a strong demand from their intended continental market – *c'est la guerre!*

## THE TRANSITION FROM REPRODUCTION TO ORIGINAL ACE

The E/1 was followed by the E/2. Although the design used the basic pressings of the E/1, this model was the first original ACE design in that the cab was extensively modified to dispense with the rather Indian 'open air' look of its forerunner. This modification also enabled each type to have a customised cab, giving them a more realistic appearance. The new loco had a 4-4-2 wheel configuration similar to its numerous life size counterparts, rather than the more exotic 4-4-4s which were much rarer on the railways of the period. The Uhlenbroch device was dropped and instead the E/2 was only available in 24Volt/DC with a new feature; an isolating setting on the control rod in the cab which enabled the loco to be parked on a live track. The E/2 was available in LB&SCR, L&NWR, LMS, NZR, Southern and British Railways liveries. The LMS livery suffered from being overcooked during the paint baking process resulting in a rather pink LMS red. Nonetheless, the LMS and the rest of the series sold well and the production run could have been doubled. Yet even then, the UK market was new and a non Hornby semi-free-lance tank locomotive was still an unknown quantity. In all, over 1300 E/1s and E/2s were produced.

Production in Taiwan ceased after the E/2, although many key subcontractors were retained and indeed still perform a vital function in areas such as gear cutting as well as tin-print sheet cutting and forming.

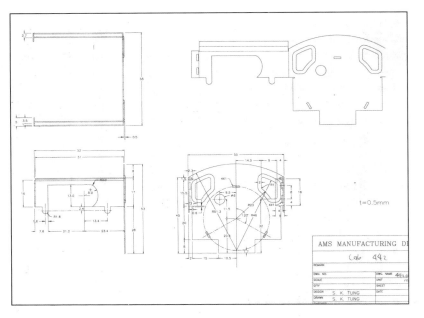

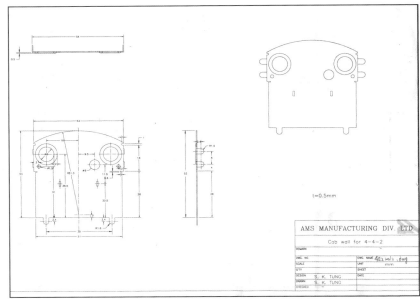

*E/2 Works drawing of Cab for tooling purposes.*

**E/2 4-4-2 TANK LOCOMOTIVE DC ONLY**
(suitable for 12v and/or 20v controllers). All DC only
equipment will be fitted with a neutral switch allowing
free-standing on live track. Production of 50 examples
of each livery.

*The E2 series which also included
an NZR type (illustrated) and a
German variant with shades of
Marklin. Our German proposer
for this model could not summon
up courage to order a minimum
quantity, such was the stranglehold
of Marklin on all things tinplate in
Germany. A pity.*
*See Page 45.*

*Both the founders had a penchant for unusual cars. After many Citroens (which I returned to), I could not resist this early 1950s Chevrolet. Our later love affair with the A4 makes this affinity with streamlined vehicles easy to understand. Andries stands proudly by his much improved Hindustani Motors 'Ambassador' Morris Oxford - for those who remember that epic of British Motoring, column gear change and all. Joining us much later, Len Mills had the most spectacular car of all; a 1930s Peugeot 302.*

*The first ACE ad in the February edition of the HRCA Journal. In view of the first ACE project, we have had a close relationship with this Association. At times this gave rise to some amusing correspondence, but in time most of those 'came to mock remained to pray'. Also shown is a fax confirming the first deliveries. With a few later deliveries and the E/2's, over 1300 E type ACE Tanks were delivered.*

*The original E/1 Mechanism showing the electronic AC/DC Uhlenbroch switching device next to lever.*

ACE TRAINS

To                                        Andries Grabowsky

From                              Allen Levy

16 March 1996

Dear Andries

Thank you for your fax of today.

OK

Batch 1

| | | |
|---|---|---|
| SR black | numbers | 80 |
| | names | 10 |
| SR green | numbers | 60 |
| | names | 50 |
| NZR | black | 15 |
| ETAT | black | 50 |
| EST | black | 30 |
| | brown | 30 |
| Nord | Green | 60 |
| | Brown | 60 |
| PLM | Red | 55 |
| D O | | 25 |

(525) ~~500~~ ~~525~~ + or - 10%

Batch 2

| | |
|---|---|
| LNER Black | 30 |
| LMS Black | 30 |
| GWR Green | 75 ~~100~~ |
| LNER Green | 40 |
| LMS Maroon | 100 |
| Metro Maroon | 100      ~~100~~ |
| CR Blue | 100 |

(475) ~~500~~ + or - 10%

Let me know your decision concerning GWR hat - Green or Chemical black so I can tell customers.

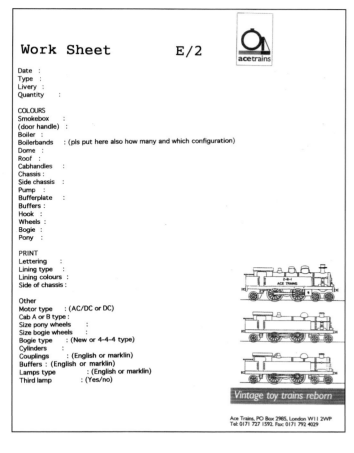

**Work Sheet**      **E/2**

Date : 
Type : 
Livery : 
Quantity :

COLOURS
Smokebox : 
(door handle) : 
Boiler : 
Boilerbands : (pls put here also how many and which configuration)
Dome : 
Roof : 
Cabhandles : 
Chassis : 
Side chassis : 
Pump : 
Bufferplate : 
Buffers : 
Hook : 
Wheels : 
Bogie : 
Pony :

PRINT
Lettering : 
Lining type : 
Lining colours : 
Side of chassis :

Other
Motor type : (AC/DC or DC)
Cab A or B type : 
Size pony wheels : 
Size bogie wheels : 
Bogie type : (New or 4-4-4 type)
Cylinders : 
Couplings : (English or marklin)
Buffers : (English or marklin)
Lamps type : (English or marklin)
Third lamp : (Yes/no)

*Vintage toy trains reborn*

Ace Trains, PO Box 2985, London W11 2WP
Tel: 0171 727 1592. Fax 0171 792 4029

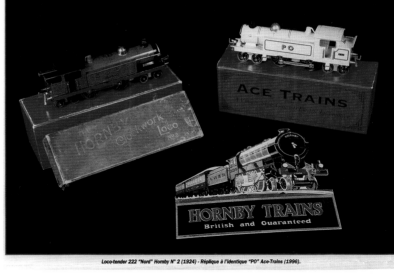

Loco-tender 222 "Nord" Hornby N° 2 (1924) - Réplique à l'identique "PO" Ace-Trains (1996).

*Early acceptance by The Meccano Group in Lyon of the ACE/Hornby replica project on their annual calendar of 1997.*

*Our dear friend Clive Lamming was always on hand to translate our various literature for the French market. Illustrated here is our leaflet for the E/2 series. Despite the impeccable French, one customer attached the rails to the mains and wondered why his locomotive was giving the impression of being a live steamer. In mitigation, he told his dealer that he had not played with tinplate trains since 1917 so had forgotten the drill.*

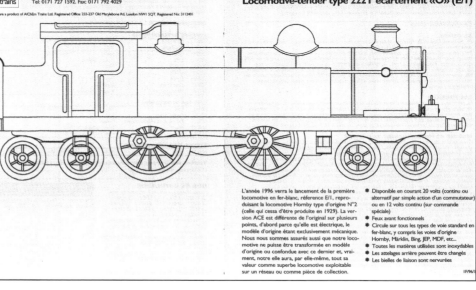

Ceci est une pièce de collection comprenant un moteur électrique de grande puissance. La locomotive ne doit pas être confiée à des enfants sans surveillance d'un adulte.

**ACE TRAINS**

**PREMIÈRE ANNONCE**
MARS 1996

Locomotive-tender type 222T écartement «O» (E/1)

Ace Trains PO Box 2985, London W11 2WP
Tel: 0171 727 1592. Fax: 0171 792 4029

...ce Trains are a product of AlChÈm Trains Ltd. Registered Offices: 233-237 Old Marylebone Rd, London NW1 5QT. Registered No: 3112401

L'année 1996 verra le lancement de la première locomotive en fer-blanc, référence E/1, reproduisant la locomotive Hornby type d'origine N°2 (celle qui cessa d'être produite en 1929). La version ACE est différente de l'original sur plusieurs points, d'abord parce qu'elle est électrique, le modèle d'origine étant exclusivement mécanique. Nous nous sommes assurés aussi que notre locomotive ne puisse être transformée en modèle d'origine ou confondue avec ce dernier et, vraiment, notre elle aura, par elle-même, tout sa valeur comme superbe locomotive exploitable sur un réseau ou comme pièce de collection.

* Disponible en courant 20 volts (continu ou alternatif par simple action d'un commutateur) ou en 12 volts continu (sur commande spéciale).
* Feux avant fonctionnels
* Circule sur tous les types de voie standard en fer-blanc, y compris les voies d'origine Hornby, Märklin, Bing, JEP, MDF, etc...
* Toutes les matières utilisées sont inoxydables
* Les attelages arrière peuvent être changés
* Les bielles de liaison sont nervurées

1F/96/1

*Original drawings by Holland Rail for the E/1 project some
time before the ACE trains arrangement was conceived.*

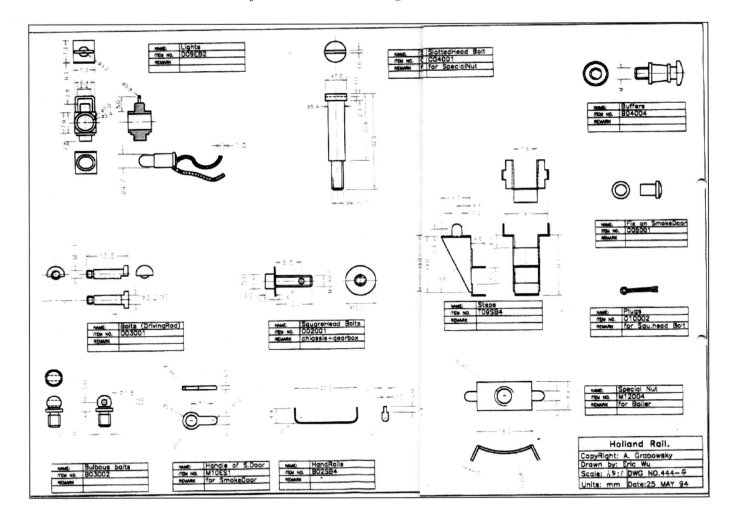

*Further original drawings by Holland Rail for the E/1 project.*

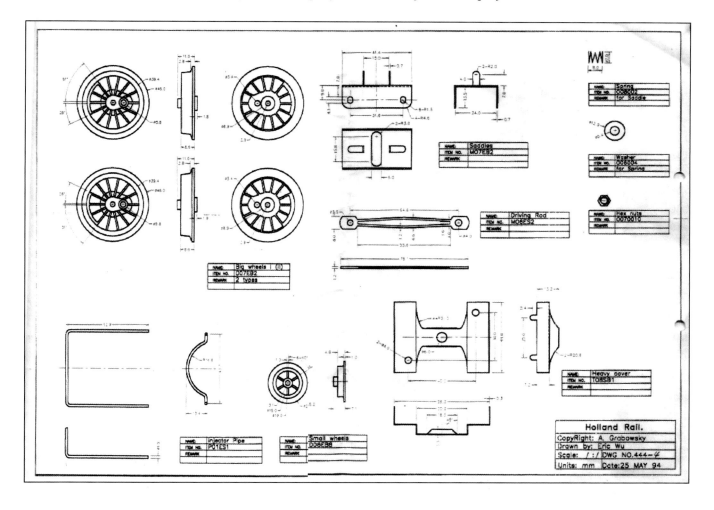

**An early report of an E/1 behaving itself in far off places.**

*And also from Ed - a report of the Seattle show at the end of November 1997.*

This last Thanksgiving weekend was the 24th running of the Pacific Northwest Region (PNR) 4th Division Model Railroad Show at the Pacific Science Centre in Seattle USA. The Science Centre is a relic from the 1962 Worlds Fair and features hands-on exhibits of Physics, Natural History, Mathematics, etc., aimed at families and children. For the train show a lot of the exhibits were moved aside to provide space in no fewer than five buildings for model railway layouts and displays. This year there were layouts in N, HO, P4, S. O scale, 027, 0 tinplate, Lego and G gauge plus various displays and demonstrations including 10-inch gauge live steam. The 0 gauge tinplate group are primarily Lionel focused but appreciate variety and I invited myself to bring and run Hornby for two of the three days. On Saturday at 9am wearing my HRCA name badge I eased my ACE E1 (I don't own a running Hornby loco yet) onto the mainline, observing the right hand running rule, with 15 Hornby and two Ridgley wagons in tow. The double track layout was a rectangular pattern approximately 16' by 20'. The procession looked a real treat and ran quiet and smoothly. Soon an audience gathered to observe the 'foreigner' show her paces. Many complements were offered. Meanwhile on the other track several US outline locomotives were having trouble getting started. The E1 ran for about an hour on and an hour off throughout the day, changing trains to provide variety. One member produced a 1936 vintage Marx Burlington Zephyr. It is roughly equivalent to the Hornby Silver Jubilee but 20V AC with seven articulated cars (coaches). The ensemble was very cheaply made of printed tinplate,

obviously a toy of the period and rattled and crashed down the track. It ran faultlessly until one axle worked its way out of the body and shorted out on the track with a goodly shower of sparks but no damage. Young children were taken with a Thomas the Tank Engine that was running on a lower loop of one of the modules. On the other mainline, families were much amused by a Lionel Action Train in pursuit of a Mickey and Mini Mouse hand car. By late afternoon I managed to invoke left hand running! Sunday was much a repeat of Saturday except for the running of a very impressive Union Pacific Big Boy complete with sound, smoke and radio control. It would overhang alarmingly on the 3-foot radius curves of the outside track. The E1 ran faultlessly for the two days. There was but one derailment, caused by a small child getting too inquisitive and derailing Mickey and Mini which in turn collided with about the third vehicle of the passing Hornby. No damage was done. The first I knew of it was hearing a great gasp from the onlooking public and then the clatter of the wagons being dragged by the E1, some on their sides, through the scenery!

I met several members of the visiting public who were Hornby-Dublo or Hornby 00 collectors and one who recognised the HRCA, but no other members.

The show was a success, with an estimated twenty four thousand paid visitors over the three days.

ATTENTION OF BOB KELLER

THE HORNBY RAILWAY

COLLECTOR February 1998

*Pacific Science Centre, Seattle*
DEPICTING E/1.

*Top: the view from the E/1 assembly room in Taipei. The original test track can be seen at left.*

*Below: the trusty Renault van that conveyed tons of parts around the City.*

*John Mayo, an extremely skilled clock maker and restorer, became an early enthusiast
for ACE and all their works. He was one of a small band of 'gurus' who were listened
to by ACE, respecting their vast experience of running gauge 0 electric trains.*

## Test Notes & Observations:

*The End Shake adjustment to the contrate wheel and motor pinion is critical.
The depthing has to be set exactly correct, to run without audible gear noise and to
eliminate stress wear engagement between the contrate and motor pinion teeth. The
average owner would not be able to do this.*

*The side shake clearance to the centre wheel pinion pivot is a little more than I would
prefer, necessary on this particular mech with some douptful gears.*

*Lubricated with "Microtime Grade H", said to be manufactured by British Petrolium Co.
retailed by Pickards of London to the horolgical and instrument industry. Available
from watch and clock material houses (suppliers).*

*This mech should now run well with any suitable oil, obtained from specialist model shops.
A long reach dispenser is necessary to reach the upper pivots and the idler pinions.
It is recommended to oil sparingly: Little and Often but never too much.*

*Avoid common petrolium based oils such as 3 in 1 which evaporates into a yellow sticky
mess after a year if left exposed in open air. This will contaminate and create abrasive
wear. WD 40 is not a lubricant!.*

*The only place where grease may be applied lightly is to the motor pinion engagement
with the contrate wheel teeth. Avoid Petrolium based grease which may harden or become
sticky.*

*The early Mech cannot run without oil lubrication, (as the instructions state) if they do they
will dot run for long and damage may have been done.*

*The common area for lubrication breakdown on early mechs, is the centre wheel pivots
which will score and seize if left dry. The first symptoms are a black powdery deposit which
when mixed with oil becomes a fine cutting paste.*

*A simple Owner Oiling Diagram is recommended when a modified example is completed for
approval.*

**The rebuilt mech is installed in a loco belonging to a member of the HRCA Wessex
Area Group where the performance can be monitored and recorded for the benefit
of the manufacturers ACE Trains London.**

**John Mayo CMBHI Mem.BWCG
Lymington**

## ACE E/1 20v AC/DC First Issue Standard Electric Mech.

**Failed Mech: Investigation, Diagnosis and Correction. @ 18 / i0 / 1999**

Faults found: Listed as detailed :-
*Corrections made as detailed :-*

1 Dead, completely ~~Seized with congealed grease~~ + oil everywhere.
*Strip Assembly, wash out + Ultra Sonic clean.*

2 No lubrication access to idler gears without removing the mech.
*Form apertures in collector shoe insulation block.*

3 Inside edge of front axle pinion touching insulation block, passing oil --
*Increase the clearance gap.*

4 Collector shoe plate close to axle pinions, too much oil will bridge the gap.
*Increase the clearance gap*

5 Rust on both centre wheel gear pivots, would cause rapid wear.
This may be the results of contaminantion from solder flux.
*Clean off and Polish the steel pivots before assembling*

6 Solder run, from contrate wheel into pinion teeth, catching the edge of the
centre wheel teeth
*Remove surplus solder to clear.*

7 Faulty gear cutting: The gear train would not spin free with the motor
removed, the wheel and pinion teeth were locking the gears would not run.
Swarf left on teeth some of which had eccentric (high spots) :- not true in
diameter. This may possibly be caused by blunt or worn cutters, or worn
machine tooling. Insufficient side shake pivot clearance, and the depthing
(meshing) set much to close for Involute teeth engagement which run best
set slack. This would certainly be the main cause of failure.
*Top and retrue the gear wheel teeth ) + increase side shake to to all
the pivots, adjust the assembled gear train to spin entirely free.*

8 Faulty electrical connections: the red pick up wire to the collector shoe
which is soldered to a brass washer was cemented to the insulator block
in super glue causing an insulated joint between the washer and the head
of the mounting screw. This was the cause of the dead motor.
*Remove superglue to make the joint live. Reverse the scew heads to the
outside, with the nuts tightened firmly on the inside, and seal with locktite.*

9 The tail of the black earth wire to the switch just pushed between the
plastic s/w unit and the steel mounting bracket, not earthing well.
*Fit the tail to the screw between two brass washers on top of the bracket.*

*It is recommended to solder the tails of all screwed terminal connections
to Terminal fixing tabs.*

**John Mayo CMBHI Mem.BWCG**

*London Toy Museum days. An electric gauge 1 Aster A4 pauses in the magnificent main station, built by the late Dave Cole, who constructed both the gauge 1 and the museum's $2\frac{1}{2}$" gauge railway in the museum garden.*

STEAM LINES No 6 SEPT 1986

NOW INCORPORATING
*Baywest City*
*The world's most sensational working model city.*

AA 'Museum of the Year' Award. Runner-up 1986.

Museum of the year 1985 — SPECIAL JUDGES AWARD

The first London Museum Project to be supported by The English Tourist Board 1984.

'Come to Britain Trophy' British Tourist Authority. 1982.

### The London Toy & Model Museum

Now established as the greatest model train museum in the world.

Apart from the collections of dolls, bears, cars etc . . . its unique garden area houses a working children's roundabout and playbus and ride-on train.

The museum is a perfect blend of education and amusement.

Admission charge. Open Tuesday to Saturday 10.00 to 17.30, Sunday 11.00 to 17.00. Open all Bank Holiday Mondays.

**The museum for all seasons and all generations.**

The London Toy & Model Museum
21/23 Craven Hill,
London W2 3EN
01-262 7905/9450

Allen Levy, the museum's founder having set off a winter service of the Flying Scotsman from Greenly Road. This gauge 1 system is one of several of the museum's working garden railway systems in steam, clockwork and electric.

*The author in a Museum advertisement c. 1986. The Aster A4 heads a train of Teak LNER coaches made by the late Ron Wheele, a long standing friend of the Author. His son Stephen, along with partner Peter Viccari, are now responsible for much of the ACE communication artwork, website photography etc.*

*Marcel and Astrid Darphin, longstanding friends and in some ways the perfect model railway couple. Marcel has always made wonderful gauge 0 railways and Astrid compliments them by creating magnificent buildings and scenery.*

*Above left: Marcel is the proud owner of ticket number 1 (being the first entrant at the London Toy and Model Museum in 1980).*

*This is not a posed picture but an amazing clash of events. The front end of the famous 'Rocket' that stood outside the museum for many years was being gingerly hoisted over the railings for installation when a vintage tour bus came round the square.*

*A bit of toy collector history when the Antique Toy Collectors Club of America were hosted in London during the summer of 1980. On the extreme left stands the late Count Giasanti Coluzzi, while in the middle is the veteran collector Ron McCrindell (in white tuxedo) and at the extreme right, your author. A magnifying glass will reveal many of the other great and good of the Toy Collecting fraternity.*

*The first of two E/1 mock ups. The second one did not survive the constant surgery it underwent.*

*Our brightly coloured PLM E/1 heads a train of AS PLM coaches at a Tuttlingen gathering.*

*The first ACE Christmas card illustrating many of the E/1 variations.*

E/1 series customers were offered the opportunity of naming their own Southern locos as a freelance homage to the real SR 'River Class' Tank locos. Illustrated here are virtually all the names applied to the class. It includes names cooked up by ACE including Virgin, Richard Branson and Mohammed Al Fayed, all designed to curry favour with their organisations. Extremely nice letters were all that materialised. I wonder where the locos finished up.

| | | | |
|---|---|---|---|
| MALCOLM S DOBBINS | MALCOLM S DOBBINS | MALCOLM S DOBBINS | MALCOLM S DOBBINS |
| CHRISTINE | CHRISTINE | CHRISTINE | CHRISTINE |
| THOMAS E HORTON | THOMAS E HORTON | THOMAS E HORTON | THOMAS E HORTON |
| WAINWRIGHT | WAINWRIGHT | WAINWRIGHT | WAINWRIGHT |
| HATCHAM | HATCHAM | HATCHAM | HATCHAM |
| DOREEN SMITH | DOREEN SMITH | DOREEN SMITH | DOREEN SMITH |
| MARGATE | MARGATE | MARGATE | MARGATE |
| RAMSGATE | RAMSGATE | RAMSGATE | RAMSGATE |
| JOHN M ABDEY | JOHN M ABDEY | JOHN M ABDEY | JOHN M ABDEY |
| ST LEONARDS | ST LEONARDS | ST LEONARDS | ST LEONARDS |
| JACQUELINE | JACQUELINE | JACQUELINE | JACQUELINE |
| MITZI | MITZI | MITZI | MITZI |
| ROGER BAILEY | ROGER BAILEY | ROGER BAILEY | ROGER BAILEY |
| DIJON | DIJON | DIJON | DIJON |
| DAVID DAY | DAVID DAY | DAVID DAY | DAVID DAY |
| CHRISTINE | CHRISTINE | CHRISTINE | CHRISTINE |
| KENLEY | KENLEY | KENLEY | KENLEY |
| SIR EDWARD SMITH | SIR EDWARD SMITH | SIR EDWARD SMITH | SIR EDWARD SMITH |
| BARNSTAPLE CASTLE | BARNSTAPLE CASTLE | BARNSTAPLE CASTLE | BARNSTAPLE CASTLE |
| LADY DIANA | LADY DIANA | LADY DIANA | LADY DIANA |

| | | | |
|---|---|---|---|
| RJ & YV GOLDING | RJ & YV GOLDING | RJ & YV GOLDING | RJ & YV GOLDING |
| BERMONDSEY | BERMONDSEY | BERMONDSEY | BERMONDSEY |
| LAURA | LAURA | LAURA | LAURA |
| JOSEPHINE | JOSEPHINE | JOSEPHINE | JOSEPHINE |
| RICHARD ORAM | RICHARD ORAM | RICHARD ORAM | RICHARD ORAM |
| FRESHWATER | FRESHWATER | FRESHWATER | FRESHWATER |
| WIMBORNE | WIMBORNE | WIMBORNE | WIMBORNE |
| BROADSTONE | BROADSTONE | BROADSTONE | BROADSTONE |
| KEN HOBDAY | KEN HOBDAY | KEN HOBDAY | KEN HOBDAY |
| WENDY HOBDAY | WENDY HOBDAY | WENDY HOBDAY | WENDY HOBDAY |
| DAVID WARREN | DAVID WARREN | DAVID WARREN | DAVID WARREN |
| BONNIE PRINCE CHARLIE | BONNIE PRINCE CHARLIE | BONNIE PRINCE CHARLIE | BONNIE PRINCE CHARLIE |
| VIRGIN EXPRESS | VIRGIN EXPRESS | VIRGIN EXPRESS | VIRGIN EXPRESS |
| RICHARD BRANSON | RICHARD BRANSON | RICHARD BRANSON | RICHARD BRANSON |
| IAN WASSERMAN | IAN WASSERMAN | IAN WASSERMAN | IAN WASSERMAN |
| MOHAMMED AL FAYED | MOHAMMED AL FAYED | MOHAMMED AL FAYED | MOHAMMED AL FAYED |
| HARRODS | HARRODS | HARRODS | HARRODS |
| HARRODS EXPRESS | HARRODS EXPRESS | HARRODS EXPRESS | HARRODS EXPRESS |
| BURTT EHRLICH | BURTT EHRLICH | BURTT EHRLICH | BURTT EHRLICH |
| JOHN JG WILSON | JOHN JG WILSON | JOHN JG WILSON | 1587 1587 1587 |

Allen, Is this what you wanted as gold rubdowns? Reg

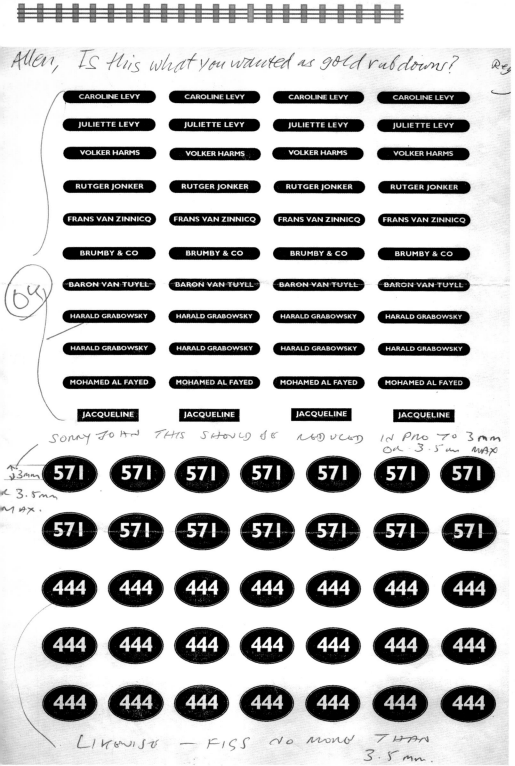

| | | | |
|---|---|---|---|
| CAROLINE LEVY | CAROLINE LEVY | CAROLINE LEVY | CAROLINE LEVY |
| JULIETTE LEVY | JULIETTE LEVY | JULIETTE LEVY | JULIETTE LEVY |
| VOLKER HARMS | VOLKER HARMS | VOLKER HARMS | VOLKER HARMS |
| RUTGER JONKER | RUTGER JONKER | RUTGER JONKER | RUTGER JONKER |
| FRANS VAN ZINNICQ | FRANS VAN ZINNICQ | FRANS VAN ZINNICQ | FRANS VAN ZINNICQ |
| BRUMBY & CO | BRUMBY & CO | BRUMBY & CO | BRUMBY & CO |
| BARON VAN TUYLL | BARON VAN TUYLL | BARON VAN TUYLL | BARON VAN TUYLL |
| HARALD GRABOWSKY | HARALD GRABOWSKY | HARALD GRABOWSKY | HARALD GRABOWSKY |
| HARALD GRABOWSKY | HARALD GRABOWSKY | HARALD GRABOWSKY | HARALD GRABOWSKY |
| MOHAMED AL FAYED | MOHAMED AL FAYED | MOHAMED AL FAYED | MOHAMED AL FAYED |
| JACQUELINE | JACQUELINE | JACQUELINE | JACQUELINE |

64

SORRY JOHN THIS SHOULD BE REDUCED IN PRO TO 3mm OR 3.5mm MAX

3mm

3.5mm MAX.

| 571 | 571 | 571 | 571 | 571 | 571 | 571 |
|---|---|---|---|---|---|---|
| 571 | 571 | 571 | 571 | 571 | 571 | 571 |
| 444 | 444 | 444 | 444 | 444 | 444 | 444 |
| 444 | 444 | 444 | 444 | 444 | 444 | 444 |
| 444 | 444 | 444 | 444 | 444 | 444 | 444 |

LIKEWISE — FISS NO MORE THAN 3.5mm.

*Also illustrated is 'John M Abday' which recently changed hands in the USA and I was able to reassure the new owner that it was genuine ACE.*

*This list is not exhaustive and in particular several PLM E/1s were named Charlotte Levy, Dijon etc.*

The good little boat 'Volta', a 23ft 'Elizabethan' that was used for many years for day sailing around the South Cornish Coast. It was on this boat that the author and Andries Grabowsky agreed to escalate the E/1 project in order to make it a viable proposition. The top picture shows 'Volta' alone in a Force 6 blow, off St Mawes Castle – almost a metaphor for the company's later plunges into the unknown with no one else in sight.

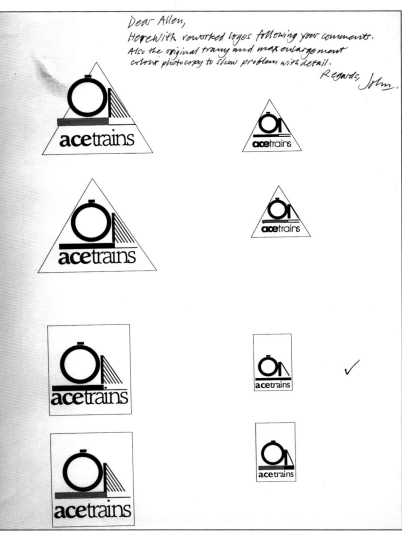

Dear Allen,
Herewith reworked logos following your comments.
Also the original trany and max enlargement colour photocopy to show problem with detail.
Regards, John.

*Visuals for the ACE logo drawn up by John Cooper.*

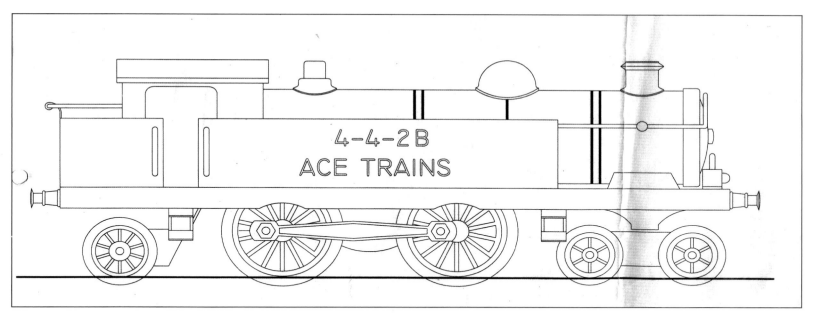

*Acceptance drawing for type A E/2. Two cab styles were available for this short lived series.*

## ACE TRAINS INDIA (P) LTD.,

8-21. MEPZ TAMBARAM MADRAS - 600 045.
Phone : (044) 2387230/31/32 Fax : +91-44-2368746
e-mail : acetrains@eth.net

*While using common logos the companies run in the Far East and London remained separate entities. Illustrated here is the Indian corporate incarnation later to become ACE Trains Ltd. In Thailand which to avoid confusion became The Vintage Toy Train Co. Ltd, when Alchem Trains was able to change its name to The ACE Electric Train Company Ltd.*

# Ace Notes

Rugby 1998 was another convivial day for ACE and its patient customers. I have recently returned from visiting the various suppliers involved with the coach programme.

The C/1 series is moving inexorably to production. A few illustrations indicate the progress being made and I was able to return from the Far East with a printed mock-up of the LMS EMU motor coach which was displayed at Rugby.

Back home I was able to demonstrate to the tin printers down at Bristol that all the parts on the printed sheet fit and that we could now safely proceed to printing all the coaches illustrated in our catalogue. In addition to those illustrated we will be supplying the LMS/EMU sets with a middle 1st/3rd coach and, for our French devotees, an SNCF coach. By the time this goes to press we will have printed all the sheets which will then be shipped for punching and assembly. With a degree of luck, some should arrive in the UK before Christmas. The long delay was caused by differences between the tooling and the proof printing, which have now been resolved.

The E/2 locos are now established and owners are reminded that the cab roof slides off allowing the mechanism to be removed more easily than is the case with the E/1.

By the time the next ACE notes appear, ACE coaches will be rolling around the world but more importantly on three rail tracks around Britain.

We have some excitement planned for 1999 but that must wait.

**Allen Levy**

PS Ian Layne comments that one of the operatives at the Cwmbran plant had been involved in Hornby 0 gauge and

*Above: Mock up of LMS Broad St - Richmond motor coach.*

*Below left: Motorised bogie gears being cut.*

*Above right: The plate pressing shop.*

*Below right: Final checks on coach brace parts.*

Dublo tinprinting at the original Caldicot works, as well as material for other toy train makers. Thus, a continuity has been preserved.

*I regularly wrote a column in the HRCA Journal under the heading of ACE Notes. Given that our manufacturing processes were not dissimilar to those of Hornby in the 1930s, the editor considered (and still does) that this contribution would be of interest to members. A few purists took exception to this for a time and when ACE items appeared on the front cover they became quite agitated. It was as if GM crops in the form of ACE were going to mutate their precious Hornby originals. The toy and model train field contatins people from all strands of life and I have had to accept that at times patience must be exercised in full. When I felt desperate about some of this I reminded myself of a line from Oliver Goldsmith's 'Deserted Village': 'Those who came to mock remained to pray'. However I exclude a certain Dr. S. from Scotland from my understanding, in view of his offensive remarks over the years. There have over the last decade been numerous reports of our demise and I would invoke Steven Sondheims' wonderful lyric: "We're still here".*

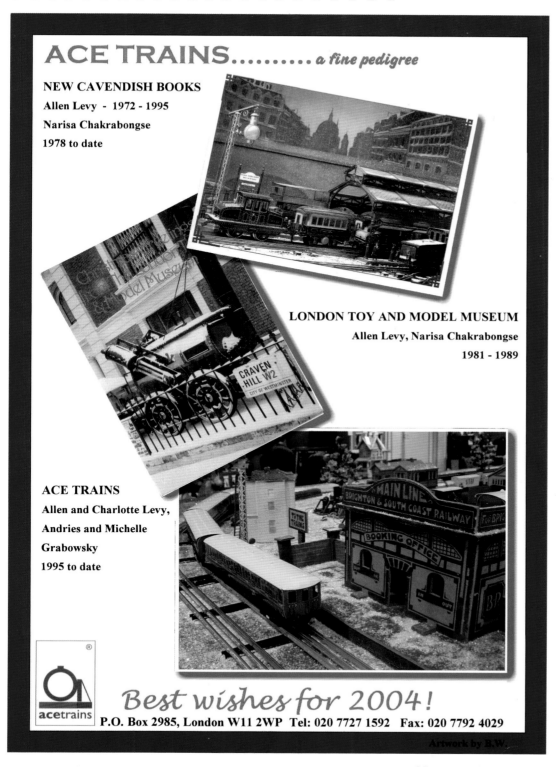

# ACE TRAINS.......... *a fine pedigree*

**NEW CAVENDISH BOOKS**

Allen Levy - 1972 - 1995

Narisa Chakrabongse

1978 to date

**LONDON TOY AND MODEL MUSEUM**

Allen Levy, Narisa Chakrabongse

1981 - 1989

**ACE TRAINS**

Allen and Charlotte Levy,

Andries and Michelle

Grabowsky

1995 to date

*Best wishes for 2004!*

P.O. Box 2985, London W11 2WP  Tel: 020 7727 1592  Fax: 020 7792 4029

Artwork by B.W.

*The long and winding road. I suppose in some ways I am a good example of the multi career ethos expounded by many economic gurus. However, apart from my days as an accountant that world never figured highly in my lexicon of things to get on with. This advertisement extolling the virtues of the ACE ancestry reflected my chameleon-like progress through the years.*

Mr Lui whose pressing works in Taipei have provided all the
sheet cutting work for ACE coaches since their introduction.
Despite requiring pin point accuracy, the works also caters for
the high precision computer business in Taiwan. Here seen with
Andries and Michelle Grabowsky discussing a recently received
sheet of LMS sides from Wales.

*Andries on crutches after returning from a long spell in a
French hospital in Limoges. Here seen leaving a restaurant
in India after his return to the fray. Christine his daughter
at right and Charlotte in background.*

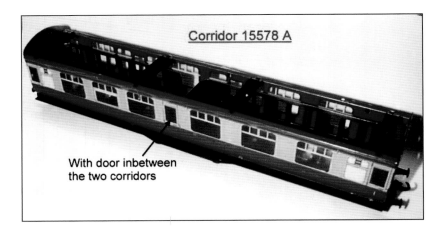

*A later production of C/5 coaches illustrates why accuracy
is so important in tinplate coach production.*

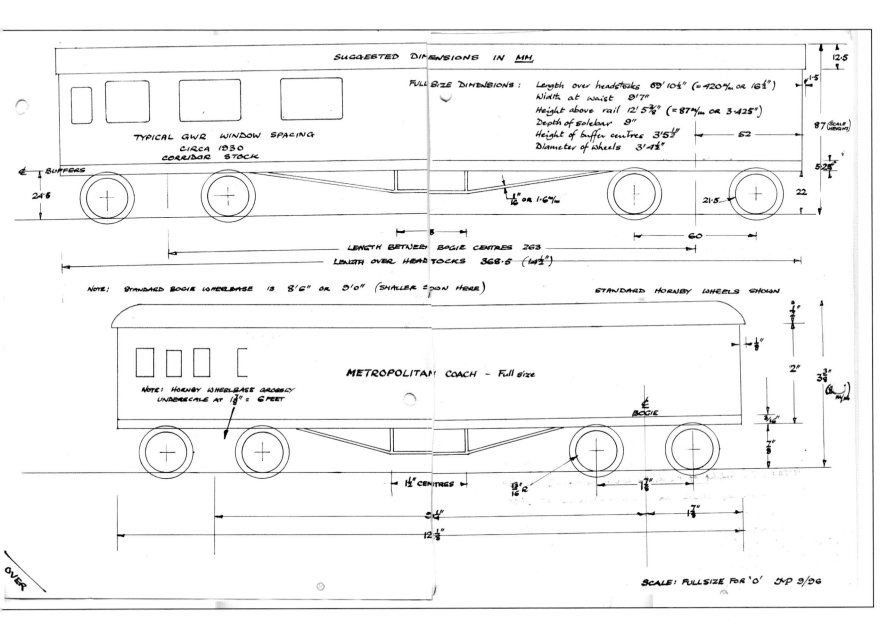

SUGGESTED DIMENSIONS IN MM.

FULL SIZE DIMENSIONS:
Length over headstocks 69'10½" (=420ᵐ/ₘ or 16½")
Width at waist 9'7"
Height above rail 12' 5⅝" (=87ᵐ/ₘ or 3·425")
Depth of solebar 9"
Height of buffer centres 3'5½"
Diameter of wheels 3'4½"

TYPICAL GWR WINDOW SPACING
CIRCA 1930
CORRIDOR STOCK

¢ BUFFERS

LENGTH BETWEEN BOGIE CENTRES 263
LENGTH OVER HEADSTOCKS 368·5 (14½")

NOTE: STANDARD BOGIE WHEELBASE IS 8'6" OR 9'0" (SMALLER SHOWN HERE)

STANDARD HORNBY WHEELS SHOWN

METROPOLITAN COACH - Full size

NOTE: HORNBY WHEELBASE GROSSLY UNDERSCALE AT 1⅜" = 6 FEET

¢ BOGIE

1½" CENTRES

SCALE: FULLSIZE FOR 'O'   JᴺP 9/96

OVER

*The late John Pentney provided us with this drawing to indicate how the Hornby Metropolitan Coach could be lengthened to c. 35 cm in order to give the equivalent of a scale 51ft which happened to be the dimension of the original Dreadnought coach on which the Hornby coach was based. This basic measurement became the norm for thousands of ACE coaches from C/1 through to C/11.*

Over the years we have sent several of our products to 'Classic Toy Trains', the leading American magazine for gauge 0 coarse scale. We have always received extremely fair comment in their product review columns. One of the first products was an LMS E/1 which recently received a very favourable long term review. Here is the loco, now the property of the magazine, at work on a typically lush layout.

## Bletchley Spring Show

Ace Trains exhibited at the Gauge 0 spring show at Bletchley and although scale rules that event (a half finished Duchess at £12000 being displayed on the next stand with a run of five all sold!) it was an enjoyable do, and I was pleased to meet Peter Bishop who showered me with information concerning the EMU sets, even pointing out that Bassett Lowke got their three car set wrong by including two and not one motor coaches. The three car set had one motor coach and a normal coach with a driver's compartment for the return journey. Having struggled to rationalise the artwork I understand why they chose that layout.

## EMU sketches

Readers might be interested in the rough sketches (illustrated below) which I have done for the EMUs. The Met type A based on the earliest units will probably not make the starting line.

Well that is enough excitement for the moment - although it is much easier to write about these matters than to produce and deliver them!

The Editor willing I shall return to these topics and hopefully have the first ACE catalogue ready for mailing.

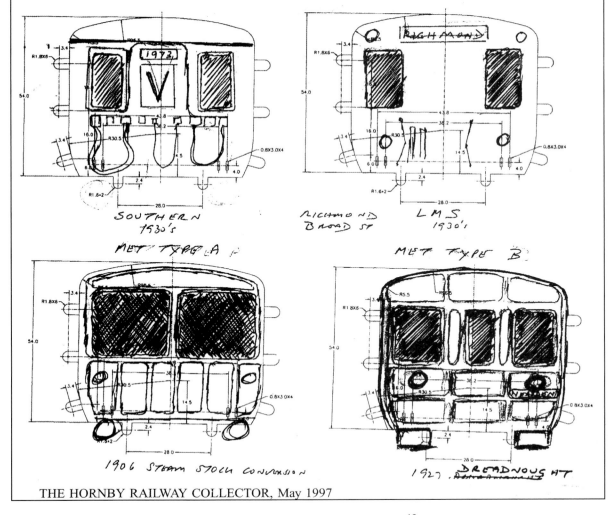

*My sketches for the EMU series as contained in an ACE Notes article published in the HRCA Journal.*

THE HORNBY RAILWAY COLLECTOR, May 1997

*Advert in the HRCA Journal which included the slogan 'Brilliantly Old Fashioned'. Photo of layout by Royston Carss.*

*The original concept for the 0-6-0 (above) using several E/1 components was discarded as the E/5 project developed under the influence of Len Mills.*

GESAMTUMBAU DER ACE-TRAINS 4-4-4 ZU EINER MÄRKLIN 2- B-1 ENGL. TYP

01 Gehäuse 4 mm höhergesetzt (Distanzhülsen)
02 Zweiter Dampfdom, beide Dome schwarz
03 Rückwand im Führerhaus, 2 Fenster, 1 Schlitz für Schaltung
04 Geländer am Kohlenkasten, gelötet
05 Pufferbohlen erhöht auf 15 mm, ca Admiration
06 Gehäuse mit Zierlinien rot und cremeweiss, Decklack Seidenglanz
07 Motor 4 mm nach hinten versetzt, Räder rot
08 Vorläufer um 7 mm verlängert, Märklin-(Darstaed) Räder rot
09 Nachläufer neu, Märklin-(Darstaed) Räder rot
10 Lampen Märklin
11 Federpuffer Märklin
12 Kupplung Märklin
13 Geländer am Führerhaus Draht vernickelt
14 Galeriestangenhalter Märklin (Bohrungen am Wassertank versetzen,Bohrungen am Kessel kleiner

*A proposed German version of the E/1 prepared by Peter Hauer. Despite its concession to Marklin, Peter became anxious that Marklin devotees would not buy it so he reluctantly withdrew from the manufacture of the batch. This model remains in the ACE archive as the reminder of what might have been A Swiss SBB- CFF variant was also drawn but never materialised.*

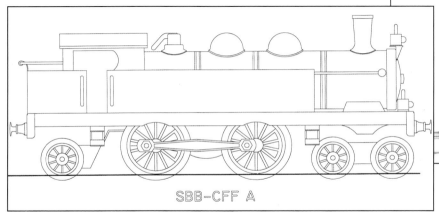

SBB-CFF A

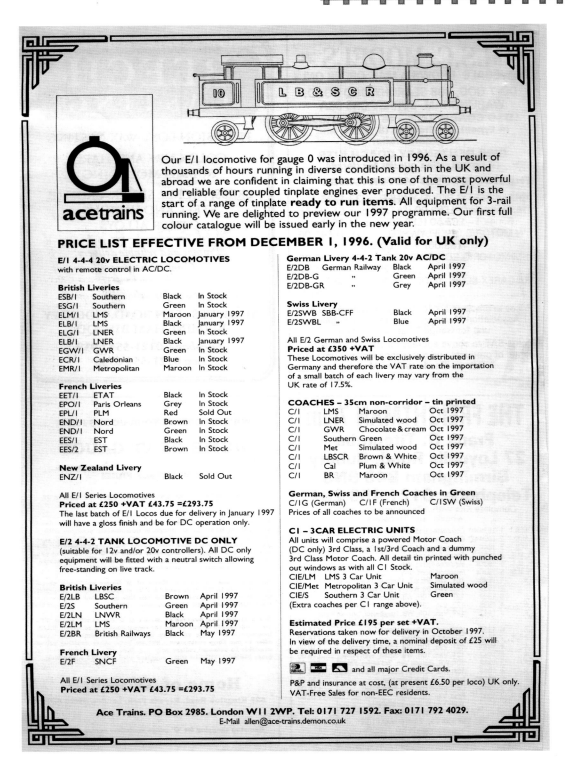

**acetrains**

Our E/1 locomotive for gauge 0 was introduced in 1996. As a result of thousands of hours running in diverse conditions both in the UK and abroad we are confident in claiming that this is one of the most powerful and reliable four coupled tinplate engines ever produced. The E/1 is the start of a range of tinplate **ready to run items**. All equipment for 3-rail running. We are delighted to preview our 1997 programme. Our first full colour catalogue will be issued early in the new year.

## PRICE LIST EFFECTIVE FROM DECEMBER 1, 1996. (Valid for UK only)

**E/1 4-4-4 20v ELECTRIC LOCOMOTIVES**
with remote control in AC/DC.

**British Liveries**

| | | | |
|---|---|---|---|
| ESB/1 | Southern | Black | In Stock |
| ESG/1 | Southern | Green | In Stock |
| ELM/1 | LMS | Maroon | January 1997 |
| ELB/1 | LMS | Black | January 1997 |
| ELG/1 | LNER | Green | In Stock |
| ELB/1 | LNER | Black | January 1997 |
| EGW/1 | GWR | Green | In Stock |
| ECR/1 | Caledonian | Blue | In Stock |
| EMR/1 | Metropolitan | Maroon | In Stock |

**French Liveries**

| | | | |
|---|---|---|---|
| EET/1 | ETAT | Black | In Stock |
| EPO/1 | Paris Orleans | Grey | In Stock |
| EPL/1 | PLM | Red | Sold Out |
| END/1 | Nord | Brown | In Stock |
| END/1 | Nord | Green | In Stock |
| EES/1 | EST | Black | In Stock |
| EES/2 | EST | Brown | In Stock |

**New Zealand Livery**

| | | | |
|---|---|---|---|
| ENZ/1 | | Black | Sold Out |

All E/1 Series Locomotives
**Priced at £250 +VAT £43.75 =£293.75**
The last batch of E/1 Locos due for delivery in January 1997 will have a gloss finish and be for DC operation only.

**E/2 4-4-2 TANK LOCOMOTIVE DC ONLY**
(suitable for 12v and/or 20v controllers). All DC only equipment will be fitted with a neutral switch allowing free-standing on live track.

**British Liveries**

| | | | |
|---|---|---|---|
| E/2LB | LBSC | Brown | April 1997 |
| E/2S | Southern | Green | April 1997 |
| E/2LN | LNWR | Black | April 1997 |
| E/2LM | LMS | Maroon | April 1997 |
| E/2BR | British Railways | Black | May 1997 |

**French Livery**

| | | | |
|---|---|---|---|
| E/2F | SNCF | Green | May 1997 |

All E/1 Series Locomotives
**Priced at £250 +VAT £43.75 =£293.75**

**German Livery 4-4-2 Tank 20v AC/DC**

| | | | |
|---|---|---|---|
| E/2DB | German Railway | Black | April 1997 |
| E/2DB-G | " | Green | April 1997 |
| E/2DB-GR | " | Grey | April 1997 |

**Swiss Livery**

| | | | |
|---|---|---|---|
| E/2SWB | SBB-CFF | Black | April 1997 |
| E/2SWBL | " | Blue | April 1997 |

All E/2 German and Swiss Locomotives
**Priced at £350 +VAT**
These Locomotives will be exclusively distributed in Germany and therefore the VAT rate on the importation of a small batch of each livery may vary from the UK rate of 17.5%.

**COACHES – 35cm non-corridor – tin printed**

| | | | |
|---|---|---|---|
| C/1 | LMS | Maroon | Oct 1997 |
| C/1 | LNER | Simulated wood | Oct 1997 |
| C/1 | GWR | Chocolate & cream | Oct 1997 |
| C/1 | Southern | Green | Oct 1997 |
| C/1 | Met | Simulated wood | Oct 1997 |
| C/1 | LBSCR | Brown & White | Oct 1997 |
| C/1 | Cal | Plum & White | Oct 1997 |
| C/1 | BR | Maroon | Oct 1997 |

**German, Swiss and French Coaches in Green**
C/1G (German)    C/1F (French)    C/1SW (Swiss)
Prices of all coaches to be announced

**C1 – 3CAR ELECTRIC UNITS**
All units will comprise a powered Motor Coach (DC only) 3rd Class, a 1st/3rd Coach and a dummy 3rd Class Motor Coach. All detail tin printed with punched out windows as with all C1 Stock.

| | | |
|---|---|---|
| C1E/LM | LMS 3 Car Unit | Maroon |
| C1E/Met | Metropolitan 3 Car Unit | Simulated wood |
| C1E/S | Southern 3 Car Unit | Green |

(Extra coaches per C1 range above).

**Estimated Price £195 per set +VAT.**
Reservations taken now for delivery in October 1997. In view of the delivery time, a nominal deposit of £25 will be required in respect of these items.

and all major Credit Cards.

P&P and insurance at cost, (at present £6.50 per loco) UK only. VAT-Free Sales for non-EEC residents.

**Ace Trains. PO Box 2985. London W11 2WP. Tel: 0171 727 1592. Fax: 0171 792 4029.**
E-Mail allen@ace-trains.demon.co.uk

*The range expands.*

## 'Decimalising an ACE', or '10 for 12'

When I collected my new ACE E12 locos, Allen Levy told me that an E/1 customer had complained that it had too many wheels. Since the customer is always right (?) ACE Trains conducted appropriate surgery to the loco, apparently to the customer's satisfaction.

Whilst I agree with ACE Trains that the E/1 will 'remain the state-of-the-art for a semi mass-produced toy locomotive for some time to come', I must say that, particularly in Southern form, it does look better as a 4-4-2T (bottom).

Since Allen kindly let me have the necessary front bogie and rear pony truck from the E/2 production, I set about the conversion for myself as follows.

The conversion requires removal of the front and rear bogies from the E/1, and replacing them with the front bogie and rear pony truck from the E/2 .

Fitting the new front bogie, which has a longer wheel base, is a straightforward replacement of the existing bogie.

Removing the rear bogie carrier requires a little more determination than if it were a Hornby loco, due to the heavier gauge steel employed. This done, the only task other than with a spanner, is to select, or make, a suitable spacer to fit in the mounting hole of the pony truck. This is necessary since the hole is somewhat larger than the diameter of the motor fixing stud over which it is to fit. This spacer (seen to the left of the pony truck in the exploded view) should be thick enough to allow free movement of the truck when the securing washer and nut are tightened down, and of a suitable outside diameter to provide lateral location. I made a suitable spacer from the terminal nut of an old spark plug, the rest of which is shown in the exploded view just above the spacer.

I hope the accompanying pictures save the proverbial 'thousand words' and demonstrate what I believe to be a very pleasing end result.

**Barry Pulford**
**Worthing, West Sussex**

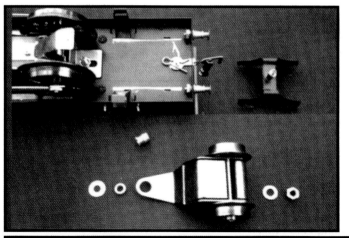

*An interesting conversion of an E/1 utilising the trailing bogie of an E/2 Such were the excellent proportions of the Hornby original it is surprising that this was not attempted by Binns Road many years before. The eventual Hornby 4-4-2 Tank was one of the ugliest creations imaginable – I should stress that is purely my view.*

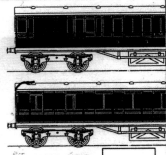

*The first ACE advert in the bastion of finescale, The Gauge 0 Guild Magazine. Many garden railway gauge 0 finescale operators have fitted insulated finescale wheels to the C/1 range in order to run this robust stock in all conditions.*

*The first showing of the C/1 range at the wonderful HRCA 30th anniversary show in Nottingham in April 1999.*

*The 30th Anniversary caps were the only headwear ever to be made at the Indian factory. Here worn by the C and E of ACE, Charlotte and Emily.*

*ACE Notes August 1997.*

*John Kitchen displaying the ACE HRCA 30th anniversary set presented to him by the Association in recognition of his long-standing chairmanship.*

*'Now, now, young lady'. I don't care if you are a member of the HRCA, you can't take pictures here.*

# Ace Notes

I was in Paris on July 3 seeing the ACE distributor 'Au Pullman' on Rue D'Amsterdam. I met up with Andries Grabowsky who was in France visiting his father. He had brought along the last EPL/1 which I had earlier returned as a non runner (loose nuts on the pick up so please note). It was immediately sold over the phone by our distributor, Lucien Demanceau. WE also dealt with a returned engine that had been on 110 volts via an ancient controller. The customer was concerned that the loco just stood and got up steam! Later that day we met up with Michel Gambin and several members of the 'Circle Ferrophile Europeen'. Also present was my old friend (and prolific author) Clive Lamming. The purpose of the meeting was to agree a French derivative for tin printing with the current production of ACE coaches. An excellent meeting and dinner at the 'Terminus Nord' and then a scoot across the road to catch the Eurostar back to Waterloo.

Sadly, a few days later I was telephoned by Andries' brother to say that Andries, his wife, daughter and father were involved in a serious car accident near Bussiere Galant close to his father's house. Harold Grabowsky - who some of you may have met last year - is in a serious condition, Andries will be on his back for at least six weeks with multiple fractures. Michelle and his daughter Christine had relatively light injuries and by now are out of hospital. No doubt by the time these notes appear in the Journal matters will have moved on and the situation altered.

I will be visiting the Grabowskys shortly and, assuming Andries is well enough, discuss the ACE programme in the light of these events.

On a distinctly lesser note I have recently recovered a substantial number of the gauge 0 locomotives stolen from my office and I would like to thank Simon Goodyear and David Thackery in particular for their prompt action in leading me to the items. They had quite innocently been purchased by a dealer in the South West who immediately returned them when I spoke with him.

Hopefully there will be better news in the next ACE Notes.
**Allen Levy**

*A selection of ACE Trains adverts.*

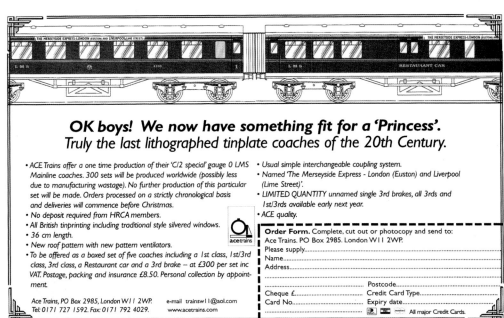

## OK boys! We now have something fit for a 'Princess'.
### Truly the last lithographed tinplate coaches of the 20th Century.

- ACE Trains offer a one time production of their 'C/2 special' gauge 0 LMS Mainline coaches. 300 sets will be produced worldwide (possibly less due to manufacturing wastage). No further production of this particular set will be made. Orders processed on a strictly chronological basis and deliveries will commence before Christmas.
- No deposit required from HRCA members.
- All British tinprinting including traditional style silvered windows.
- 36 cm length.
- New roof pattern with new pattern ventilators.
- To be offered as a boxed set of five coaches including a 1st class, 1st/3rd class, 3rd class, a Restaurant car and a 3rd brake – at £300 per set inc VAT. Postage, packing and insurance £8.50. Personal collection by appointment.

- Usual simple interchangeable coupling system.
- Named 'The Merseyside Express - London (Euston) and Liverpool (Lime Street)'.
- LIMITED QUANTITY unnamed single 3rd brakes, all 3rds and 1st/3rds available early next year.
- ACE quality.

Ace Trains, PO Box 2985, London W11 2WP.
Tel: 0171 727 1592. Fax: 0171 792 4029.
e-mail trainsw11@aol.com
www.acetrains.com

**Order Form.** Complete, cut out or photocopy and send to:
Ace Trains. PO Box 2985. London W11 2WP.
Please supply.....................................................................
Name.................................................................................
Address.............................................................................
.........................................................................................
.................................... Postcode........................................
Cheque £.............................. Credit Card Type.......................
Card No............................... Expiry date.................................
All major Credit Cards.

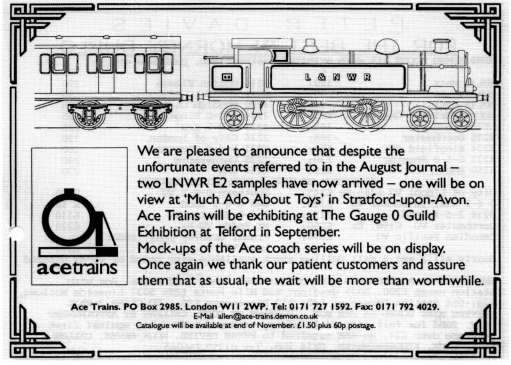

We are pleased to announce that despite the unfortunate events referred to in the August Journal – two LNWR E2 samples have now arrived – one will be on view at 'Much Ado About Toys' in Stratford-upon-Avon. Ace Trains will be exhibiting at The Gauge 0 Guild Exhibition at Telford in September.
Mock-ups of the Ace coach series will be on display.
Once again we thank our patient customers and assure them that as usual, the wait will be more than worthwhile.

**Ace Trains. PO Box 2985. London W11 2WP. Tel: 0171 727 1592. Fax: 0171 792 4029.**
E-Mail allen@ace-trains.demon.co.uk
Catalogue will be available at end of November. £1.50 plus 60p postage.

*My reflections on the Tambaram factory project.*

## Ace Notes

### The C/1 Project

I can open this column again as those who attended the 30th Anniversary junket in Nottingham will attest that C/1 coaches finally emerged. They in fact arrived at around noon on 16th May and were promptly labelled and transhipped to Nottingham that afternoon.

Before saying anything more about the coach saga I must state what a wonder the 30th Anniversary celebrations were. The .ayouts were exceptional from Bernard Cook's mega gauge 0 polis through Chris Reeve's Baykoland, Frograil in fancy dress and Chris Graebe's circle of rarities- to name but a few. Can I be forgiven for saying that the absolute gem was the Meccano grotto which was simply magical, including a Raylo set described as 'somewhat scarce'.

Since my last mini bulletin regarding Andries I am pleased to say he was allowed back to his wonderful factory in Madras. After joining him for a week we both returned to Europe, he to attend his father's funeral (typically his urn was laid to rest next to a French branch line) and I to London to await delivery of the first batch of C/1s.

Those of you who took delivery of your HRCA coaches will know how far the bits and pieces had been sourced but the crucial point was the final assembly in the factory at Tambaram, Madras. To say that the assembly area resembled Binns Road in the 1930s is not an exaggeration. Substitute ladies in overalls for ladies in Saris and there you have it. Days before delivery the crucial bogie casting would not eject cleanly from the tool. Endless polishing coupled with much patience eventually solved the problem.

Thus, apart from the scale of operations I think I have experienced the procedures that Binns Road would have gone through to produce a tinplate bogie coach. One thing is certain; nobody at Binns Road or Tambaram was thinking this finish or that would give rise to learned articles in the Journal half a century on. Virtually everything that happens in a train factory does so on the hoof. Thus the back-up diecasting firm completing the outside bogie frames was close to a powder coating factory resulting in the HRCA coaches having black bogie sides. The original diecaster whose tool only came on stream at the last moment preferred a chemical blackening finish which was applied to the other liveries shown at Nottingham. This latter process will probably become the standard for the main run, albeit in a darker finish. I well remember being at Binns Road during the final days when Thunderbolt aircraft were being sprayed and being told about the problems of paint batches and colours generally.

When an HRCA coach was found to have the couplings put on upside down it was immediately rectified at Nottingham. If a brand new Hornby coach turned up like that, articles would appear in the Journal asking whether anyone else had seen one! Perhaps given a few years all this might change and the matt finished pre-production E/1 bodies that lie around my office will become objects of great debate.

The great thing for me was to watch the C/1s spinning around the reproduction layout in room 13 - most of the time on two foot radius curves. Thank you Charles Henry and team for your enthusiastic showmanship.

I thought a photograph of part of the production process in India would be of interest. Shades of Meccano Magazine in the 1930s.
**Allen Levy (577)**
**Ace Trains**

*A project to provide a compatible new base for a Hornby Metropolitan to run as a Bo + Bo using an ACE motorised bogie and trailing bogie was caught in the move from Madras to Bangkok. It has remained in the warehouse in Bangkok awaiting a few final parts while other larger production took its slot. It will however emerge if only to keep faith with customers who have inoperable original Met locos. This sketch gives the general idea of what is proposed.*

*Emphasising a small company's ability to cater for small but enthusiastic markets is this E/2 New Zealand set ordered by Railmaster Exports in Auckland. Several of the locos were damaged in transit to New Zealand although some were repaired but nonetheless down the years this will become a very collectable item for all the right reasons. It was not to use that awful term a limited edition but a small run that became even smaller.*
*A black E/1 version is also illustrated.*

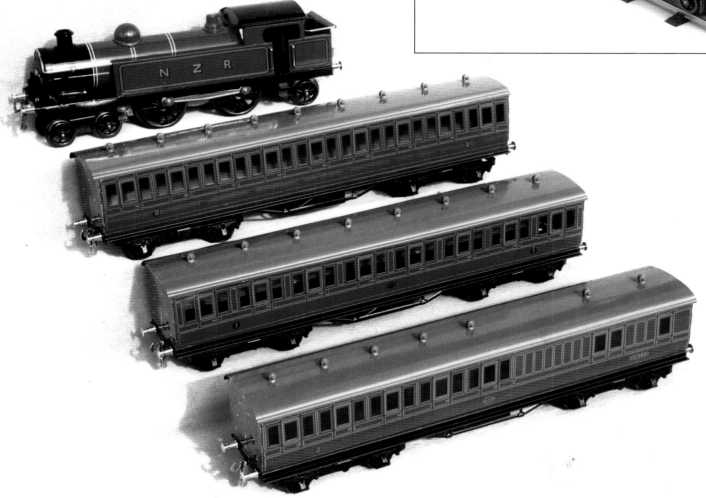

*Scenes at Luffs printing works during production of the C/1 range. This association unfortunately came to an end when a batch of sheets came to grief. I remember this well as I stayed on in Wales to pass this sheet and missed a stage performance of Nicole Kidman in 'The Blue Room' back in London that night. Many years later the Tourist Stock emerged as the C/10 stock.*

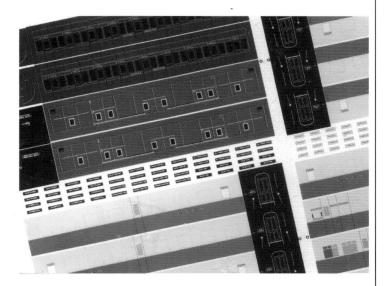

To                    Rob Christmas

Ace Trains
P.O.Box 2985
London WII 2WP
Tel: 020 7727 1592
Fax: 020 7792 4029

From                  Allen Levy

December 14 2000            fax and hard copy

Dear Rob

At approx 1 10 pm the package from Luffs arrived.

Given that they were allowed to choose the sheets of their choice our case is made.Not one sheet matched and on coaches nos 43503 and 4350-4 a distinct light cast appears at the left hand side.

The Green on both these coaches is a different shade to nos 43501 and 43502.

The Buffet Car is again a slightly lighter shade than 43501 and 43502. As a boxed set these differences would be visually exçacerbated leading to the problems we had in the first printing. It was knowledge of that printing that led my Associates to be very cautious before spending further money on this printing.

*An extract from our regrettable parting shot with Tinplate Reproductions*
*The reference to the first printing refers to the rather wayward colour of the*
*lower panel of the LBSCR C/1 coaches. Had it not been for the fact that tinplate*
*LBSCR bogie coaches had not been produced by any of our predecessors more*
*problems would have arisen earlier.*
*Nonetheless Rob Christmas was instrumental in our first faltering steps in*
*resurrecting Gauge 0 tinprinting and we will always have good memories of our*
*visits to Bristol and Wales in pursuit of our goals.*

*The 'controversial' front cover of The Journal depicting an ACE EMU. A full version of this very popular set is also illustrated.*

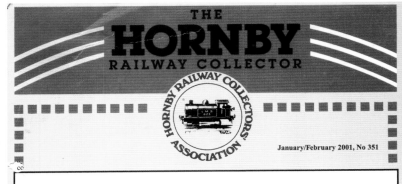

THE
# HORNBY
RAILWAY COLLECTOR

HORNBY RAILWAY COLLECTORS' ASSOCIATION

January/February 2001, No 351

*1996-2000*

# SERVICE LETTER No 1

## Subject: 'Hot Box' condition in E/1 locomotive mechanisms.

Where relevant this letter supercedes the original pink instruction sheet.

*Part of the learning curve of resurrecting ready-to-run three-rail gauge 0 was listening to users' comments. This first service letter relays things learnt after the first period of operation.*

It has come to our notice that some of the early issue of these locomotives are not running properly at slow speeds. This may be caused by a lack of lubrication on the gear train axles where they protrude through the chassis frames.

To test for this condition run the loco for a short period (say 15 minutes) then remove from the track and touch both motor chassis frames, if they are warm or if a screeching sound was heard during running, then the following action should be taken before any further running.

Obtain a small quantity of light car engine oil, (the residue of a used 1 litre top-up pack will be sufficient). This can be drained into a small screw topped glass jar. You will also need a fine sable hair artists brush (No. 0 or 1) and a magnifying glass.

To gain access to the gear train, the mechanism must be removed from the loco body. In the absence of a 7mm box spanner you will probably have a spare Meccano spanner, but unfortunately, it will not fit as 7mm hexagonal nuts are used on the mechanism and the rear bogie. That old Meccano spanner can be filed to fit.

Unscrew the brass control knob and place it in a saucer which will also be handy for the other nuts and washers.

Invert the loco onto a soft cloth or duster and insert a piece of rigid plastic (size 56mmx70mm) inside the cab roof. This is to protect the paintwork on the underside

when removing and replacing the mechanism. The end of the control rod can cause damage if this is not done.
(This also applies to DC locomotives where the rod operates the isolating switch).

It is advisable to remove both bogies to give easy access to the nuts that hold the mechanism (make a note of the order of nuts, bolt, washers and springs on the bogies). Likewise note the position of the wiring when removing the mechanism.

Carefully detach the red wire from the front end of the motor to complete the separation.

You will see that the brass gear train is well greased, but the ends of the axles are clean. Every one of these axle ends must be identified and oiled carefully with just a small amount on the brush. Some axles can be done from the outside through the driving wheel spokes. It is advisable to apply the same treatment to the driving wheel axles, bogie axles and springs, and crank pins.

Care must be taken to avoid any oil being spilt on the motor drive shaft.

Remove any surplus oil with absorbent tissue.

Re-assemble in reverse order taking care not to trap any of the wiring under the mechanism mounting plates.

Please note that the revised blue instruction sheet for mark 2 motors is still valid.

*Ace Trains, April 1998*

**E/1** will be available in several British, French and New Zealand liveries as listed. This series of engines will be produced in one production run only, after which a locomotive based on the 2711 No 2 locomotive is planned. As production of individual liveries will be limited, early ordering is recommended for specific liveries. A limited number of Southern locomotives, ie ESB/1, ESG/1, will be offered with a personalised name at no extra cost. This offer will only be open for orders placed before the end of March 1996 on which full payment has been made. This offer is strictly limited to availability and a number of prior registrations have already been received. Names should be limited to 17 characters (including spaces).

## SPECIFICATION

### Body

The body is made of tinplate and some items such as the boiler and watertanks have been made of thicker materials than the original.
To utilize the extraordinary power of the motor, extra weight has been added to the watertanks to give maximum traction. The locomotive is some 30% heavier than the original clockwork version. The base plate has been thickened to add rigidity. All diecast items such as lamp holders, chimneys etc are cast in an Australian zinc material which is 99.9% pure – (so its safe to put one away for your grandchildren without worrying about the dreaded 'crumble').

### Paint Finish

The paintwork has been executed according to the best processes available. The paint is of Swiss manufacture. Where primer has been applied it has been baked on for 30 mins at high temperature. A further high temperature lacquering process is applied for a further 30 minutes after which the lining and printing (including where relevant the various crests) is applied. After this a varnish is applied for a further 30 minutes at 150 degrees C.

### Motor and Autoreverse

It is in this area, in particular, that this locomotive will differ from Gauge 0 Hornby electric products. The engine is fully operational both for AC and DC running, and in the AC mode it has a similar autoreverse function to the original Hornby reverser. E/1 is compatable in all operational details with the original Hornby or later tinplate standard track. The motor is a 24V DC motor that will start to work at 4 volts. It is brushless and will not require maintenance. The motor is five pole and at 12V makes approx 9800 rpm and at 20V approx 16400 rpm (without load). High torque (twice that as recommended by the Gauge 0 Guild) will ensure slow and fast running under load without stress to the motor. The maximum current consumption (including running lights) is about 0.7 amps. which enables the use of even the most simple transformer, whether AC or DC.
All locomotives are fitted with a device (custom made in Germany) that converts AC supply from the rails to a DC supply to the motor incorporating the autoreverse feature as in pre-war Hornby electric locos. This device can be activated for AC supply or deactivated in case that supply to the rails is DC, by means of a push/pull rod in the cab. As the engine only draws a minimum amperage, the controller must have the Max-Off-Min-Max arrangement when autoreverse function is used in the AC mode. If using a Hornby T20 or T20A transformer then this will have to be coupled to a resistance controller/circuit breaker (see page 244 *The Hornby Gauge 0 System* by Chris Graebe). A 12V DC version will be available to special order only – at no extra cost.

## Wheels and Drive

All wheels are manufactured from diecast zinc and coloured black by chemical process. The wheels are a faithful reproduction of the original, but the driving wheel flanges have been adapted to modern standards so that the engine will negotiate both vintage and modern three rail points. All gears are in brass and all shafts in tempered steel. Gears are pre-greased and will not require oiling, only an occasional touch of grease, this to avoid undue oiling of track surfaces. All gears are mounted within a stainless steel housing giving a clear view through the driving wheel spokes. The accuracy of the gear train is assured by cutting the shaft location holes by laser. Centre-rail pickup via Hornby style sprung collectors, made of nickel plated brass for optimum conductivity and longevity.

## E/1 LOCOMOTIVE AVAILABILITY

### British Liveries

| | | |
|---|---|---|
| ESB/1 | Southern | Black |
| ESG/1 | Southern | Green |
| EMB/1 | LMS | Black |
| ELM/1 | LMS | Maroon |
| ELB/1 | LNER | Black |
| ELG/1 | LNER | Green |
| EGW/1 | GWR | Green |
| ECR/1 | Caledonian | Blue |
| EMR/1 | Metropolitan | Maroon |

### French Liveries

| | | |
|---|---|---|
| EET/1 | Etat | Black |
| EPO/1 | Paris-Orleans | Grey |
| EPL/1 | Paris Lyons Mediterranee | Red |
| END/1 | Nord | Brown |
| EES/1 | Est | Black |

### New Zealand Livery

| | | |
|---|---|---|
| ENZ/1 | NZR | Black |

**All priced at £249** (inc VAT) plus £6 p&p UK only

**ORDER FORM**

Please supply locomotive(s) - Tick box
- [ ] ESB/1  [ ] ESG/1  [ ] EMB/1  [ ] ELM/1
- [ ] ELB/1  [ ] ELG/1  [ ] EGW/1  [ ] ECR/1
- [ ] EMR/1  [ ] EET/1  [ ] EPO/1  [ ] EPL/1
- [ ] END/1  [ ] EES/1  [ ] ENZ/1
- [ ] Standard 20V AC/DC
- [ ] 12V DC – delivery date on request

Special naming offer. PRINT NAME CLEARLY

...................................................................

I enclose my cheque/postal order for:

...................................................................

Ace Trains PO Box 2985, London W11 2WP
Tel: 0171 727 1592. Fax: 0171 792 4029

**PLEASE STATE WHICH CARD YOU ARE USING**

Please debit my Access/Mastercard/American Express/Visa account

Card No:

Expiry Date:

Name

Address

...................................................................

Post Code

Signature

*Details of the first E/1 instruction sheet.*

Hornby SCALE MODEL OF

"Princess Elizabeth"

Gauge O

20-VOLT ELECTRIC
LOCOMOTIVE WITH TENDER
AUTOMATIC REVERSING

*Hornby's artwork of the late 1930s was very similar to the longer C/2 coach issued by ACE some 60 years later. The LMS Hornby coaches as issued bore little resemblance to the illustration above.*

# Hornby RAILWAY COLLECTORS' ASSOCIATION

HORNBY RAILWAY COLLECTORS' ASSOCIATION

THIRTY HRCA YEARS (logo please)

There are a further 20 rakes of the Ace Trains 0 gauge coaches available owing to a low wastage rate at the factory. Many members will have seen examples of the three coach rakes (comprising 1st, 2nd and brake/2nd) at the 30th Anniversary Convention in Nottingham and they are of the same high standard we expect of Ace Trains. They bear the THIRTY HRCA YEARS logo and are finished in a crimson lake/maroon shade with yellow lining; the price of £150 includes an attractive and strongly made presentation box. They are fitted with drop-link couplings and self-compensating bogies with cast metal wheels. They are available through the Association only until the end of this month (May). The cost does not include postage, packing and insurance. Orders must be received by the Treasurer by Saturday, 29th. May 1999 and should be accompanied by a cheque, made payable to the H.R.C.A., for £150; orders will be accepted on a first come, first served basis and it would be appreciated if applicants include an S.A.E. for a reply. These Anniversary coaches represent a true limited edition since less than 100 will have been produced.

Mike Dove 16-4-99

*Although designed to fill the gap in the late 1930s Hornby Coach range particularly for their Princess locomotive the C/2 was more than a match for any LMS tinplate loco of the period.*

# LMS Corridor stock 1933-39

From the end of 1932 when Stanier became chief mechanical engineer LMS carriage design underwent a further change. Although timber ... y framing was still used, steel panels formed the outer skin of sides, ends and roof. All protrusions such as window frames were eliminated. The cumbersome drop window and rotating glass ventilators were replaced by fixed windows and sliding window ventilators, features which are still standard on the latest BR stock. Illustrated RIGHT and BELOW is an open third; similar designs were evolved for side corridor stock, of both first and third class, and brake vehicles.

[British Railways

*Mike Allen, a long term friend of ACE Trains, offering his meticulous advice which more often than not led to revisions of our manufacturing processes.*

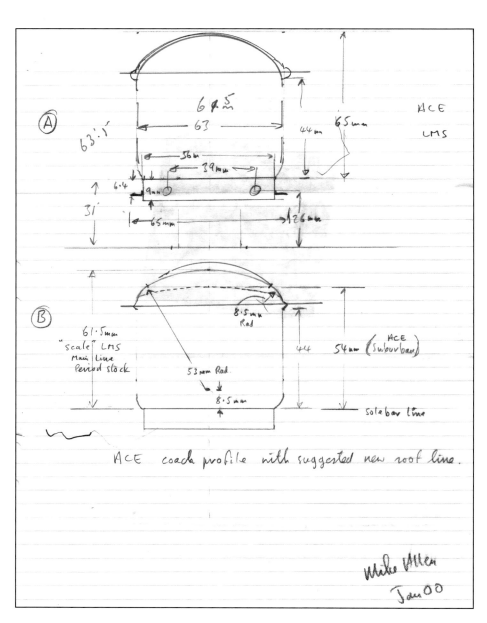

ACE coach profile with suggested new roof line.

Mike Allen
Jan 00

The C/2 Merseyside Express series proved to be a great success despite doubts about the shape of the roof. Various observations on this are illustrated together with a rather misleading picture of the real thing. Possibly the roofs were too domed but they certainly made up for the lack of stature of similar offerings by Hornby in the 1930s. Seen with a Hornby compound (page 59), in my view one of the best Hornby offerings. Also looking quite good with a Bassett-Lowke Railways issue Mogul. (Above)

Although Hornby incorporated lighting in many of their accessories they never fully mastered the scaling down of lights in their locomotives and rolling stock. Illustrated is the first rear light set offered with the C/1 range. Though distinctly tinplate in scale, it captures the spirit of the tail lamp. Later these were fitted as standard on some sets. A series 2 light was developed for the second series E/4 and this was fitted to all brake ends from set C/4 onwards.

Lima of Italy made an assault on the gauge 0 market but for British users chose a slightly smaller scale, making their products incompatible with existing stock. Here, a lima mark 1 full length coach in 1/45th (65 ft) contrasts with a 40 cm ACE pre-production sample 1/43rd scale (c.61ft) GWR coach.

# CHAPTER TWO – 1996–2000: THE MADRAS INTERLUDE – C/1s, C2s AND EMUs

## INDIA

In 1996 it was all change. Andries and his wife Michelle moved to India to set up a factory making hats for the Japanese market, with tinplate train assembly as an ancillary activity. The factory was located in an economic zone known as Tambaram (MEPZ), near the airport of Madras (now Chennai), and was financed by Andries and his brother-in-law. Rows of sewing machines were installed, staff trained and samples made before an ailing Japanese economy led to the cancellation of the contract. It is amusing to reflect that the only paying customer this venture ever had was ACE trains with its order for 1000 caps, some of which were presented at the HRCA 30th Anniversary dinner at Nottingham in 1999.

So, a large factory designed for hat production became available and rather than occupying one part of a floor, ACE was now able to spread out over three floors. It was from that factory that well over 10,000 printed tinplate coaches, specifically the C/1 and C/2 range, later emerged. The decision had already been made to produce a whole range of tin-printed British – and in the event, French – coaches. We settled on a length of 35cm which would equate proportionally to a real life length of 51ft. The particular coach chosen as a generic pattern was the 'Dreadnought' type used on the Metropolitan Railway. This basic concept was to prove the blueprint for all ACE coach sides right from C/1 through to C/11 and will still form the basis of any future 35cm that feature a 'tumblehome' side panel.

## REVIVING GAUGE O TINPLATE PRINTING

The problem that faced ACE was how to resurrect the black arts of producing tin-printed gauge 0 coaches after a period of some 40 years since serious mass tinplate production had ceased in the UK with Hornby, Mettoy and Chad Valley. Enter Ian Layne, the guru of tin-printing history. He was aware of a burgeoning business in printing decorative tins for biscuits and other confectionery requiring the 'old fashioned' look. An introduction by Ian to Rob Christmas of Tinplate Reproductions and their reproduction house in Bristol before long re-established a vintage chain of contacts including Luffs in Wales, who had last printed coaches for Hornby's Dublo range in the 1950s. Given my background in publishing and my long association with John Cooper, our freelance designer at New Cavendish Books for over 15 years, the problem was addressed. In the late 1980s the

computer was beginning to take over many of the manual tasks of the graphics industry. John, a self confessed Luddite in the field of graphics, had to undergo a sea change in his methods. Whereas all the vintage producers of tinplate used graphic artists to create meticulous, hand painted artwork which would then be exposed onto film before transferring to photo sensitive litho plates, the computer would generate these images onto CD Rom discs and the information was then digitally transferred (even down phone lines – a very big deal in those days) to film thence to the printing plates. So the brush became the keyboard and the whole process was transformed. I dwell on this topic because it is a classic case of new technology reviving old processes. An interesting aside to all this is that some of the original artwork for the C/1 series was commissioned in the old fashioned way from Roy Fearn, who was the principal supplier of overlays for customising or restoring Hornby Dublo tin-printed vehicles at that time. Roy produced the artwork for the Metropolitan coaches, EMU and the LNER C/1 range. In the event only the LNER hand painted artwork was used and this range remains as a reminder of the 'old art'. Hand painted artwork had been used to create thousands of images that were turned into tin-printed plates but its time had come to yield to a far superior and more flexible technology. It is inconceivable today that anyone would attempt to produce a factory batch of printed tinplate railway stock using the old method. So collectors take note: The LNER C/1 represents a 'fin de siecle' product.

## FRENCH C/1s

The C/1F series comprising coach sets for the Etat, PO, Nord, Est and SNCF did not strike the same chord as the locomotives. Sales were slow and quite a number of Nord coaches were converted into three-car German Triebwagens, which were originally ex-Prussian stock taken over by the French as part of their share of First World War reparations. Some were merely converted for use as German stock, given the dearth of German made tinplate vehicles of this type and price. A generic baggage van was also issued, circa 1999, based erroneously (in that we followed another strange colour) on a small French production by a firm called Nolfa – a bud that never blossomed.

**acetrains**

GAUGE 'O'

*Ace Trains fait part de la disponibilité de cinq nouveaux coffrets une rame de trois voitures des réseaux suivants: PO, Est, Nord, Etat et SNCF, toutes basées sur le style des fameuses voitures "Ty" de la "Belle époque" avec plusieurs classes chacune. Ces voitures sont un sommet jamais atteint dans la qualité des voitures tinplate à bogies offertes sur le marché français. Seulement 100 rames de chaque réseau ont été produites. En supplément un fourgon à bogies de style traditionnel français est disponible dans une livrée verte courante.*

Tous les coffrets sont proposés aux prix de **FF 1.900**. Le fourgon est proposé à **FF 550**.

Nous avons en stock notre célèbre série de locomotives-tender, référence E/1 du type 222, fonctionnant en courant 24 volts continu ou alternatif. Ces locomotives sont disponibles dans les livrées suivantes: PO (gris), Est (brun et noir), Nord (vert et brun), Etat (noir). Toutes ces locomotives sont proposées à **FF 3.000**.

Toutes le matériel ACE est doté d'attelages interchangeables avec ceux d'autres marques. Tous les bogies sont de type français exact (avec des roues à rayons de type exact) et ces bogies sont du type compensé offrant de ce fait des possibilitiés de démontage facile pour l'entretien ou le changement aisé des essieux.

Nous faisons une offre spéciale comprenant une locomotive et une rame plus un fourgon pour **4.900 FF** (frais d'envoi compris).

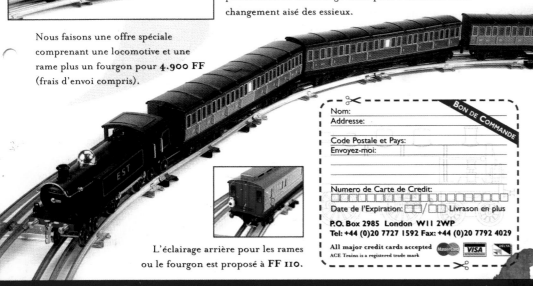

L'éclairage arrière pour les rames ou le fourgon est proposé à **FF 110**.

**E m a i l :  t r a i n s w 1 1 @ a o l . c o m    W e b :  w w w . a c e t r a i n s . c o m**

*Despite a slow start ACE has established itself as the only active supplier of gauge 0 tinplate to the French market. The products of AS which at times has been confused with ACE in the French pronunciation has since its demise in the early 1990s acquired a new status with prices for some items surpassing those of Jep and other earlier French makers. Illustrated here is the very popular C/1 Est Set and the Nord Set which has been highly sought after by German operators. It can easily be redesignated as the original Prussian type it was before it went to France as reparations after WW1.*

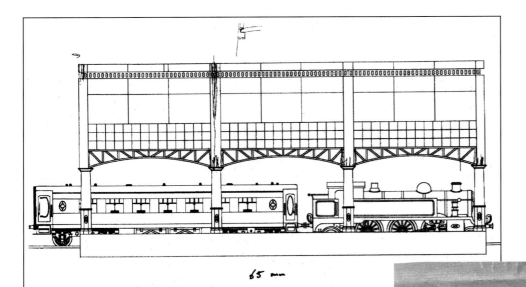

65 mm

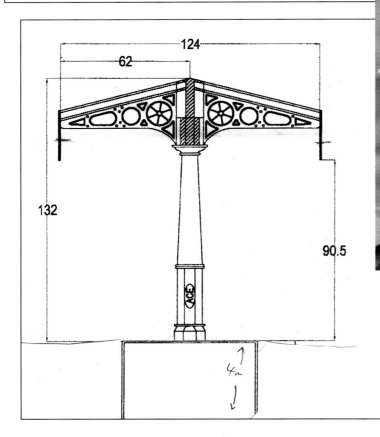

124
62
132
90.5

ACE

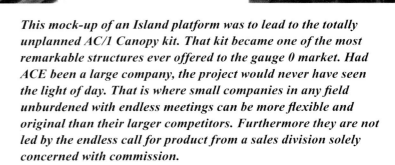

*This mock-up of an Island platform was to lead to the totally unplanned AC/1 Canopy kit. That kit became one of the most remarkable structures ever offered to the gauge 0 market. Had ACE been a large company, the project would never have seen the light of day. That is where small companies in any field unburdened with endless meetings can be more flexible and original than their larger competitors. Furthermore they are not led by the endless call for product from a sales division solely concerned with commission.*

**Pre-production mock-up of the Canopy "Well it all fits – but will it sell?".**

As with the Nord C1s in Germany, many of the baggage vans were converted to become the basis of the ACE/Wright Line, which proved to be highly successful and rarely in stock for any length of time. I will return to the ACE/Wright connection later.

Having established ACE Trains as the leading maker of 1/43 tinplate-style trains in Europe, we are now completing the range of French 35cm coaches with a five car rake of PLM coaches, perhaps the most colourful of all French passenger stock. These are due for issue in early 2006. We produced a quantity of PLM E/1s in what can only be described as alarming red but nonetheless remains relatively true to the extremely rare Hornby versions of the 1920s. A bucolic meal in Paris may well have been the original cause of that choice – we will never know. Needless to say, I have not discovered whether the real PLM ever had such flights of fancy. At this point I should mention the excellent Czech firm of ETS. This company has a prolific output but has chosen a scale of 1/45 and are not strictly speaking compatible with the ACE line.

### ACE EMUs

Another line in the C/1 series were the three C/1E sets, namely The Metropolitan (Baker Street – Harrow), the LMS (Broad Street – Richmond) and the Southern EMU set. A new motor bogie was developed for these multiple units which has been remarkably virtually trouble free since its inception in 1999. The AC/DC facility was retained but this time a PC board with a bridge rectifier replaced the somewhat temperamental Uhlenbroch device. An added feature was an isolation position on the rod system – a weakness particularly in the hands of certain postal services where the Taiwan sourced switch tabs were not up to very rough handling. The AC system was manual in that once selected, reversing was accomplished by moving a control rod. In DC these units operated by remote control. As with the C/1 series, producing these units were a logistical nightmare. The sheets were printed in Wales then shipped to Taiwan for cutting, plastifying and forming, after which they were sent to India for assembly before being boxed up and transported back to London. This period was a tribute to Andries' genius for outsourcing everything from boxes to motor parts. I witnessed this while spending the whole day in a dirt floored foundry the size of a one car garage outside Madras, waiting for a pair of bogie castings to come out cleanly from a mould being heated with charcoal and urged on by bellows.

### TROUBLE IN T' RAJ

One significant sub-contractor for ACE were the Suba Brothers of Madras, who made many of the base plates for C/1 production. Charm oozed from them as they promised 500 C/1 bases for the next day only to find that during the previous evening a better prospect had turned up. This resulted in our being confronted the following morning with a floor covered with fan pressings and not an ACE base plate in sight. Our dark maroon boxes, used for the majority of our Indian made product, suffered from Indian inks that proved to be far from permanent. On top of all this, manufacturing in an economic zone meant that every nut, bolt and screw had to be checked in, and likewise every item leaving. Towards the end of our stay a more fluid arrangement was arrived at with the help of strategically delivered bottles with Scottish connections. It was not that any vast sums of money where at stake, but simply that Indian bureaucracy had reached unheard of proportions and time was rarely of the essence. Endless chits and chalans in India and similar time consuming paperwork in the UK is one area of globalisation that small businesses can do without.

India is a paradox in that it is fast becoming one of the IT centres of the world but in low-tech production it does not offer any easy route for manufacturing exporters located there. A similarly paradoxical position was to be found during the next ACE move to Thailand whereas most of Europe bends over backwards for inward investment, certain countries in the Far East take the opposite view.

### FILLING A HORNBY GAP –
### LMS COACHES FOR A 'PRINCESS'

Our last 'hurrah' from India was the C/2 five car 'Merseyside Express' set. Although our email links formed an indispensable part of ACE communications, low cost office scanners had not yet come of age. In the case of the C/2 roof production this led to a verbal misunderstanding as to the amount of curve required. In the event, the LMS coaches resembled those illustrated, but not produced in Hornby's 1937 *Book of Trains*. These coaches were meant to fill a gap left in Hornby's range when they introduced their 'Princess Elizabeth' Pacific, so it was a case of art following art rather than William Stanier. Nonetheless, apart from one or two adverse comments by the inevitable experts, the C/2 sets proved to be good sellers and, like most of the Indian-made ranges, are no longer available

# Ace Trains - Another Milestone

Or would it be more appropriate to write that April 29th represented another milepost?

On that date I met up with Allen Levy at the Bristol premises of Westgraphics to view the first tin-printed sheets of Ace rolling stock to come off the proofing press prior to being sent for tooling trials. These first-off samples were the designs for the LMS EMU formation and we were not disappointed by their colour rendering, depth and crispness. If this is maintained on production runs the ACE coaches will rank among the highest standards seen on the tinplate tracks.

In his catalogue Allen mentions that the rolling stock series will be printed by a printer having connections with the production of Hornby tin-printed stock. Perhaps it is opportune to explain the historical significance of this connection. In fact, there are two separate paths of genealogy from the Hornby tinprinting work carried out at Caldicot Printing Works near Newport over a period of three decades, commencing in the mid-1920s.

The Morgan family had an involvement at Caldicot at this early stage and tinprinted items as small as the Platform Luggage and as large as the Engine Sheds. In 1932 they moved over to Bristol to found Avon Tin Printers with a facility for tinplate fabrication as well as tinprinting pure and simple. The present owner of Westgraphics was works manager of Avon Tin for many years prior to its take-over and closure in 1990.

Westgraphic's function has been to convert the computerized artwork of John Cooper into printable format on metal, produce the 'progressive' printing plates for the build up of the overall patterns and to initiate the proofing runs to ensure the desired end product and repeatability of quality.

Production runs will be carried out at the Cwmbran works of Cyril Luff Metal Decorators Ltd. Luffs had a later involvement in the Caldicot story before taking advantage in post-war years of the facilities offered by the Cwmbran 'new town'.Completing the third side of the triangle mention must be made of the invaluable advice and assistance given by the present operators of Caldicot Works, namely Linpac Metal Decorators. Linpac's main operation is at Reading, formerly the well known firm of Huntley Boorne and Stevens. It was to them that the first approach was made and they had great interest in the historical connection, However, as I suspected, their production runs tend to be geared to hundreds of thousands (or even several million) compared with our more modest requirements. Nevertheless they gave valuable advice in identifying suitable preparatory and production printing channels as indicated in the foregoing text. The Hornby connections just seemed to drop into place. Perhaps a good omen for success!

**Ian Layne**
**Long Ashton, Bristol**

*Allen Levy (left) and the author inspect the first-off proof sheet for the ACE Trains tinprinted coaches.*

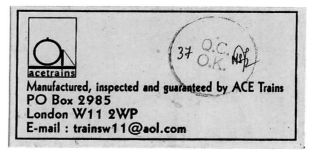

*ACE has developed a small network of dealers throughout most of the UK. One such firm was the famous coach making company of Edward Exley resurrected by Quentin Lucas.*

*Ian Lanes contribution to the ACE revival of lithographic tin printing for gauge 0 material was invaluable.*

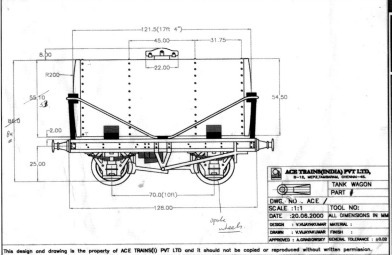

The Petrol Tanker series was first conceived in the Indian period and this drawing depicted the production wagons that would emerge many years later. Alan Brown was instrumental in providing much of the original artwork from this extensive collection of vintage petrol tankers. The later milk tanker series was interestingly based on a Dutch built tank wagon as illustrated below. Some years later when the Tankers were finally issued an ACE Oil Tank Wagon was added to the series. Milk Tank Wagons including an Express Dairy version were added to the start of the goods stock that will be developed by ACE.

3,000 Gallon Glass Enamelled Milk Transport Tank

# ACE TRAINS – 1st Series Tank Wagon Programme

ALL METAL FOR GAUGE 0-3 RAIL (2 RAIL OPTION WILL BE AVAILABLE) INTERCHANGEABLE COUPLINGS

ex-stock. A later by-product (assembled in Bangkok) were the even more popular C/3 kits, when left over parts from the C/2 production were made available as kits, complete with chopsticks for turning the tabs. This idea was borrowed from the production procedure in Taiwan for turning tin tabs. This tradition was carried forward with great success to the Indian factory.

These kits were a throwback to the Burnett tin toy kits of an earlier time. It should be mentioned that by this time a C/3 roof had been developed with a lesser curve. Retailing at £35, nearly 800 kits flew away, and so Hornby's rather modest mainline LMS coaches now had a worthy successor.

## SETBACK

1998 was a sad year for the ACE project when Andries Grabowsky was involved in a near fatal accident while visiting his late father's house in the Limousin in Central France. It was Andries' extremely strong constitution that helped him pull through and despite a degree of infirmity he returned to the ACE fray as boisterous as ever – anybody who has ever met him will recognise that engaging and occasionally enraging part of this remarkable character. Yet he is without doubt a genius in the field of model train production.

## THE FINAL INDIAN PROJECT – UNFULFILLED

As a post script to India's role in the ACE story one should mention the ill-fated LNER Tourist Stock project. This proved to be our sad farewell to Welsh tin-printing for ACE. During tin-printing, I would attend the factory in Cwymbran (it was always raining) to approve the sheets prior to the actual run. In the case of the Tourist Stock, I approved the colours and assumed they would apply on the printing run. I left to return to London and several weeks later received a call from Taiwan, where the printed sheets had been sent for cutting. They told me that the colours varied from one side of the sheet to the other. This was potentially disastrous as these coaches were destined to be sold as a six car set.

The project was scrapped when random sections of the sheet were seen in London. In 2005 a new series of Tourist Stock was revived, this time as a six car set with correct articulated units, proving the old adage that some things are meant to be. These sets, known as C/10, are already being marketed and are, of course, part of the Bangkok production era.

*The test track in Taipei used to see if ACE equipment would run on the roughest layout with a mix of various makers points all in dubious condition. Here an E/1 seen with various Hornby stock.*

*Summit meeting on beach, close by Pondicherry in Southern India. It was here that the C/1 coach programme (over 11,000 units) was determined.*

*An early meeting in Taipei with a resin manufacturer to explore the possibility of fabricating the A4 body in resin. A rather wonderful paper model of an A4 is on the table. Fortunately this avenue did not lead far.*

*Many years later, we bit the bullet and cold diecast the A4. The problem of lining the smoke box was finally solved with the adoption of decals. Previously these were masked and sprayed in this most difficult area of the A4.*

# ACE TRAINS

*Vintage Gauge 0 Trains*

## C/1 First Series: Non-Corridor Coaches

ACE COACHES DESIGNED IN LONDON

ASSEMBLED BY ACE TRAINS (INDIA)

TIN PRINTED IN WALES

An ACE British boxed set comprises three outline coaches – a full 1st with eight compartments, a full 3rd with nine compartments, and a 3rd brake.

Dimensions are based on the 57ft 'Dreadnought' coaches, and the 36cm length of the coach represents virtual scale proportions in gauge 0 (approx 7mm = 1ft).

Illustrations show actual pre-production models.

TOOLING MANUFACTURED IN TAIWAN AND SWITZERLAND

The coaches are fitted with compensating bogies, the outside frames attached to the inner frame by two screws. Wheels may be easily changed by removing

one outside frame. A circlip retains the ACE coupling, and these may be changed for other makes by removing the clip and withdrawing the pin.

These coaches have been extensively tested on most proprietary tracks, and will run perfectly on track down to 2ft radius. Single C/1 coaches will be available later in the year.

The hole at the rear of the 3rd brake is designed to take an Ace Rear Light set, which will become available as an accessory in Autumn 1999.

Further coaches are planned for release next year.

TIN PLATE REPRO MADE IN BRISTOL

DIECAST ZAMAC FROM AUSTRALIA

TIN PLATE MADE IN UK

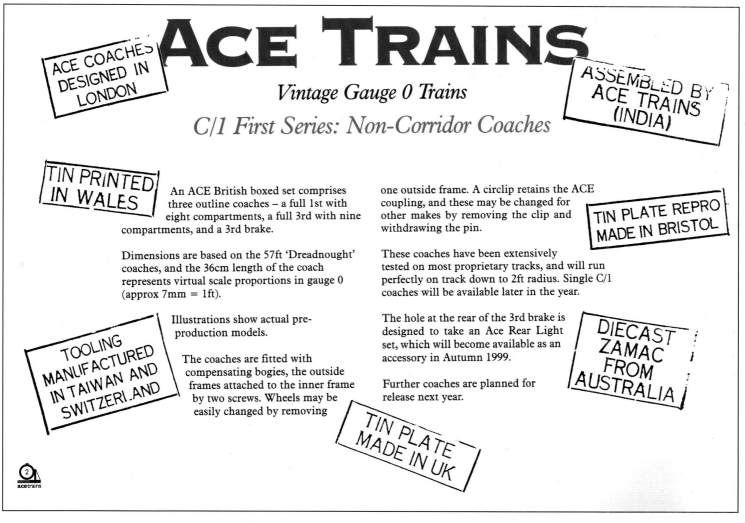

2
acetrains

*The notion that specialist tin printing can just be fed into a factory in the Far East at one end and emerge as saleable items in practical quantities is a myth. Sourcing materials and sub-contractor is vital to an operation such as ACE. Whereas we have not been problem free with this approach we have not encountered the disasters that have befallen some gauge 0 makers both here and abroad. This illustration from our Indian produced C/1 range illustrates this diversity.*

# CHAPTER THREE: BANGKOK, WIDENING HORIZONS, A4s AND ALL THAT

## THE BANGKOK ERA BEGINS

And so, in 2000 the ACE operation moved with the Grabowsky family to their next port of call – Bangkok. At this stage in the ACE story the role of the ACE wives should be mentioned. Michelle Grabowsky was originally destined to run the hat factory in India and so by default found herself in charge of the ACE Thailand office administration in Bangkok, while in London, Charlotte Levy took control of distribution to customers worldwide. Her cheerful voice soothed many an anxious customer, whose long awaited ACE treasure was finally consigned to the tender mercies of Parcel Force and other shippers.

The production unit was always separate from the London operation. There were no cross shareholdings, just a series of agreements that one part of ACE Far East would supply, and ACE London would buy one hundred per cent of all products destined to be sold under the ACE registered label. Despite all the vicissitudes already touched upon, this arrangement between The Vintage Toy Trains Company registered in Thailand and The ACE Electric Train Company Ltd (formerly Alchem Trains Ltd) has continued over ten years. Whilst not exactly a marriage, the arrangement has (despite some reasonably torrid 'philosophical' differences) remained solid where other more lawyer based agreements have foundered. Andries Grabowsky still retains the Darstaed name, which he threatens to resurrect one day, and that line does not form part of the gentleman's agreement concerning ACE products. I have little doubt that when those 40 cm Marklin manqué coaches roll off the line ACE London will be involved in the marketing at the very least.

A major undertaking was moving the tooling and inventory from India to Bangkok, but it was achieved – at first to one location then to a dedicated ACE factory.

By a quirk of Thai company law, my son Hugo (celebrated Thai actor and media personality by day, demon rock star by night) found himself President of the Far East production outfit. He is well qualified for this in that he has a large gauge 0 railway in the basement of his mother's house in Bangkok. Reports filtering back from visitors suggest this three-track layout resembles a speedway, in that ACE locomotives and rolling stock are subjected to electrifyingly fast running. In some ways this aids the ACE project as anything that survives the dreaded basement in Chakrabongse House will probably function for many years in kinder hands.

A new work force was recruited and trained, then production of the C/4 LNER Teak and C/5 BR Mark 1 – 'blood and custard' coaches began. Some components shipped over from India were still used, but various tools couldn't be adapted for use in Thailand. Taiwan was still the centre for gear cutting, tens of thousands of which would be required for the E/4 ( A4) project but also as a manufacturing base for roofs as well as sheet punching and forming.

## INDIAN LEFT OVERS – THE METROPOLITAN BASE

One long term project (not through intention) was an Indian pre-slotted base for an original Hornby Metropolitan body. The base was designed to allow the Hornby shell to operate as a BO+BO but regrettably it still lurks, awaiting a box and a few straps for attaching the body. Like most ACE projects they will eventually come to the market but delays are part of a culture where delivery times do not support any attempt to organise lean methods of manufacture. Most of the major train makers of the world operate out of one factory in China, but that form of manufacture would not suit the rather bespoke nature of the ACE project. Our production can be improved on the run, a luxury not given to the disciplines of large scale production. Thus, frustrating as it may seem at times, the mitigation is that, on the whole, a far more charismatic and thought through gauge 0 product comes forward when every aspect of production is under a dedicated management. Imagine Morgans being produced by one of the major car factories – it simply would not have the same cachet.

Thailand has no history of making metal gauge 0 trains so the learning curve started on the base line as far as component makers were concerned. Into this void stepped Andries Grabowsky and Vijay Velappan Kumar, chief engineer of the Madras outfit and instrumental in organising the C/1 production line, who joined the migration to Bangkok.

Furthermore the E4(A4) project was the first major locomotive to make a quantum leap from the E/1s and EMUs that went before.

*BR A4 'Bittern' in her last days in service up in Scotland. Taken on a business trip during my accountancy days in the early 1960s.*

*Andries admired a super detailed ACE Triebwagen at work at the 2003 Tuttlingen meeting. An Elettron FS Pacific can been seen at right.*

*ACE A4 rushes through ACE double canopy with new Gresley teaks (black window variant)*

ACE Trains 'ACE DAY' at Wimbourne's Bi-annual Railway Show, April 26 2003

Three rail Gauge 0 tinplate always wins at Public Exhibitions, so we thank Alan Seymour and his merry men for giving the good folk of Wimbourne a great show.

*'this is what I really want, Dad'*

ACE Trains has become a sub-culture and in this advertisement an ACE day in Wimborne, Dorset is being illustrated. ACE equipment forms the basis of many a public running session, making all day running more practical than was possible with vintage equipment not in the hands of owners who were able to regularly service them. Here one should pay tribute to the late Ron Grayson, who for many years applied his considerable expertise to maintaining tired vintage mechanisms.

*Cock o' the North*

72 Newton Crescent
Dunblane
Perthshire
FK 15 0 DZ
20th December 2003

Dear Mr. Levy,

Although I have only spoken to you on a couple of occasions by telephone, I thought that this time I would commit pen to paper.

The purpose of this letter is to express my delight and complete satisfaction of the Gresley Teak and MK1 'Blood & Custard' coach sets, which (through your Scottish agent – Dale Smith) I have recently taken delivery of.

I have to say that everything about these new coaches is perfection personified and makes them a most desirable quality product. The coaches, along with the A4's, will undoubtedly become collectors items in their own right.

For too long the 'O' gauge tin plate scene has been decried by those who view it as something from the past but, thanks to ACE, a quantum leap has been made in its revival and rightly so. I am sure there are many of us who will thank you for that.

I expect you will have been inundated with many suggestions from customers with their *wish lists* as to what to make next, so will not bore you with mine. Suffice to say that what you have produced so far has been *spot on* and well worth the wait. If its LNER and / or a design classic I am happy !

So once again many thanks for a superb product range – my only problem is in keeping up with items while they are still available.

With all best wishes and every success for 2004 and beyond.

Yours sincerely,

*David Woods*

D W WOODS
HRCA 6444

I had on display a total of nine 4-4-4 locos (5 ACE, 4 Hornby) and invited chatty, interested people to look at the lineage. Your new 'blood and custards' stood (when they were not running) next to a Hornby 4-wheel blood and custard - some contrast.

There was a great deal of interest throughout the weekend. The great bulk of visitors are adults with young families, who come along on a family ticket. They are not looking to buy, but they are the toy train runners of the future.

Of course, it was the ACE Caledonian and coaches that drew the most admiring comments up here. The combination looked lovely, and ran extremely well. Your coaches 'sit down' so well - not a single coach derailment on tricky tinplate track in 15 hours of running. And thank you for going for drop-link couplings; no trouble from them either.

All I need now is some other nice, shore wheel-based ACE locos to sit alongside my Hornby 2711 locos and my 4-4-0 compounds. What chance of another ACE loco with four driving wheels and no outside motion other than coupling rods, eh? Your 4-wheel motors run beautifully, and on the move your 4-4-4 and 4-4-2 engines look superb. And for people like me, with only a small running track here at home, they look entirely right with 3-coach trains. I would love to add some ACE 4-4-0 locos of some sort or other to my collection and to my running operation. I sense that quite a lot of other people would like that too. Just an idea!

Anyway .... thanks for all that you have done and all that you are doing. You've added a new dimension and a great deal of extra pleasure to the way in which I operate within this particular hobby.

Best wishes

Robert

Robert Wilson

HRCA 1299

*Apologies to the writer in the HRCA Journal whose name has been mislaid.*

## Tin - and affordable!

I have been collecting principally Hornby and other tinplate for over 35 years and in that time have acquired only seven bogie coaches, because even all those years ago I considered the price asked to be too high, so you can imagine what I think now. This is mainly the reason why I scratch-built so much.

Then along came ACE Trains. I ummed and arrhed until it was nearly too late and then in a short space of time nearly trebled my stock of bogie coaches and added two locos to the shed. Why? Because they are made of tin and are affordable, even to me. I know of at least one case of someone starting collecting on the strength of the price and quality of ACE. Now, that can't be bad, can it? I eagerly await the future.

Touching on red distants; it is surprising how little railway modellers, and especially collectors, actually know of prototype practice.

*One of the more gratifying aspects of running ACE Trains is customer feedback. One of our early testimonials came from Richard Lines of the famous Lines Brothers family (Tri-ang etc) who on running his Southern E/1 and C/1 Coaches wrote to us and said that 'Frank Hornby would have been proud to have made the ACE range'.*

Dear Alan, The 'train set' arrived safe and sound this morning - Tue. They really are the most wonderful products Alan - congratulations! A train set for Christmas! the first time since 1952.

*Jim - Diane Crombie*

I do wish you all a good event and much regret not to join you to share in your landmark achievement. In my opinion Ace Trains have now come to equal Hornby Trains in their heyday of the 30's for variety and quality. So congratulations and look forward to the next decade of your runners.'

all regards
John Haworth

*Extract of letter received from John Howarth October 6 2005.*

Coaches were less of a problem as a standard matrix of manufacture had been established in India and this could very easily be transposed to Thailand.

## A4 (E/4) – THE QUANTUM LEAP

The A4 (E/4), however, was an entirely different proposition. Having decided to manufacture this fabulous machine in 7mm scale the next problem was how to make it. Could the body be a pressing? Could it be lost wax and etched brass as made in Korea? Or could it be cast, as was the Hornby Dublo with their legendary pre-plastic production from 1938 onwards. Bassett-Lowke had of course built A4s in tiny quantities around the same time as Hornby introduced Dublo in 1938. They were amazingly expensive and surprisingly, the bodies were extremely crude when viewed from underneath. More to the point, they were virtually hand made and nowhere in the Far East could this type of production be sourced at a sustainable price. The nearest thing would be to assemble a kit and that would drive the costs beyond what a newly revived market could bear. Furthermore, soldering techniques were not commonly used in Thailand. The twin requirements of robustness and superb traction could only be achieved by giving the locomotive immense power and the maximum weight over the driving wheels – this and a draw of no more than one amp under full load. These were the parameters drawn up in 2001.

Drawings were completed and an old Douglas fibreglass locomotive was acquired just to get the feel of shape, if not the exact measurements. From the detailed drawings a wooden pattern was made, from which an aluminium shell was cast. That shell was then used for dimensional purposes and to build a mock-up of the chassis. It had been decided that the body would be cast in pure mazac and fitted to an all geared chassis driven by two matched motors – a first in steam outline gauge 0 three-rail, at least as far as a factory assembled model was concerned. A long visit to Bangkok was made to settle further details and also to inspect the body tool, which measured over a square metre and had to be lifted by an overhead hoist. Early attempts to extract clean castings from this large casting were frustrated by rapid cooling of the metal in certain flow paths. Eventually the tool was modified and trial castings were able to be produced. A further unique feature of this production was the fitting of micro-bearing to all shafts and axles.

## HIGH LIFE IN PICCADILLY – CHRISTMAS AT FORTNUMS

Many months of development followed and by Autumn 2002 two working prototypes were ready just in time to be thrust into a gruelling schedule of running six, and later seven, days a week. This took place on the now legendary ACE layout set up in the famous tea room on the fourth floor of Fortnum and Mason in Piccadilly. The layout was designed by Alan Brown and manned by a rota of enthusiasts on a daily basis. The layout was an enormous commitment in time for a small company such as ACE but it proved to have many long term benefits. Nothing like it had been seen in Central London since the great Christmas layouts at Gamages in Holborn during the 1950s, and even then they were principally equipped with Lionel material. The ACE Fortnum and Mason layout opened to the public for three months running up to Christmas 2002.

The two pre-production A4s, Mallard and Sir Nigel Gresley, ran for over 200 real miles during their stay at Piccadilly. Apart from some lubrication and several valve gear failures (notably on the same side) the general assemblies held up well but several modifications resulted from this trial of strength. It took nearly two years of production to achieve the bulk of the run, which by early 2005 totalled over 850 units, with several colour variations still to complete. Sales of the E4 locomotive were worldwide with strong sales in France, Australia and New Zealand. Sales in America were handled principally through an arrangement to supply 'Golden Eagle' with a set of Coronation Coaches, via Weaver Incorporated. They also sold the ACE Canopy AC/1 on an exclusive basis in the USA. Production finally ended in 2005 and in view of the historical importance of this venture, I am including a table of all the types made and, as far as possible, the names and variations. As I write, a live steam version is under development in association with the renowned live steam engineer John Shawe. It may be of interest to note that the ex-Fortnum and Mason Mallard has been offered up as the test bed for the sample version which, if successful, will lead to the production of the first high pressure gauge 0 steam locomotive ever offered in batch production. Furthermore a two-rail electric version of the E/4 is being developed.

As with the history of ACE, not every twist and turn was premeditated. In one of our countless email and telephone call exchanges, Andries announced that he would like to insert a station canopy into our burgeoning programme. It would be wrong to say that my first reaction was positive.

*Before the arrival of British Railway Modelling, Railway Modeller was the predominant monthly magazine. However the almost total absence of editorial and articles concerning coarse scale gauge 0 was palpable. When an RM guide to getting started in the hobby proclaimed that there was virtually no ready-to-run material gaskets blew. The resulting letter ensued.*

Ace Trains
P.O.Box 2985
London W11 2WP
Tel: 020 7727 1592
Fax: 020 7792 4029

The Editor
The Railway Modeller
Beer
Seaton
Devon
EX 12 3NA

December 24 2002

Dear Sir

I refer to your 'Beginners Guide No 1 Getting Started' page 10 '0 gauge'.

I appreciate that your Magazine has long been in denial as to the existence of three rail gauge 0. I accept the fact that if that is your editorial policy then as publishers of a highly successful journal that is your absolute right however much it may alienate some of your readers.

However when you publish 'factual guides' the criteria shifts and facts become more relevant. The writer of your 'Beginners Guide ' displays remarkable ignorance of what has been going on in the world of Gauge 0 railways in the last 6 years.

ACE Trains have produced over 10,000 British outline 51ft scale scale coaches which could be used for three rail or with a simple procedure two rail operation. They covered virtually every region of the country both pre grouping , Big Four and BR, all ready to run. If as you suggest Bachmann's Brass Coaches were 'ready to run' you do not help inform your 'beginner' one jot.

ACE have also produced a large line of Tank Locos some freelance some more prototypical plus three EMU three car units. We have recently introduced a Station Canopy in metal and glass that any beginner could assemble in 2 hours with no particular skills other than the use of a screwdriver and spanner. We are about to introduce an A4 locomotive which will probably be the equal of anything made by the great manufacturers of the past and will leave most existing models of this iconic locomotive standing for performance and appearance. At the moment it is for three rail but a two rail version will be introduced in 2003. We have been the leading manufacturer of British outline ready to run gauge 0 for years.

All this information has been widely available over the last 6 years and I suggest the authors of your 'guides' research a little more widely before writing 'factual guides'.

Yours faithfully
Allen Levy
Managing Director – ACE Trains

Ace Trains are a product of AlChEm
Train Ltd. Registered Office:
233-237 Marylebone Rd, London
NW1 5QT. Registered No: 3112401
Ace Trains is Registered Trademark

EMAIL: trainsw11@aol.com • WEB: www.acetrains.com

## ACE TRAINS
### - *Overlay Series* -
Designed and prepared by
**Brian Wright**

One of the more profound tipping points (to use current jargon) was the introduction of Brian Wright by Alan Brown to ACE. What has emerged from this collaboration is a series of artwork for both the tin printed ACE range and also for the ACE/Wright overlay series which has enabled very special bogie vehicles to be produced that could not justify a tinprinted run. Also illustrated is the Dynmometer Car issued with the C/8 Record Breaking Set, one of Brians most celebrated pieces of artwork.

*The ACE/Wright series has enabled us to produced highly specialised vehicles, which could not otherwise justify a full production run.*

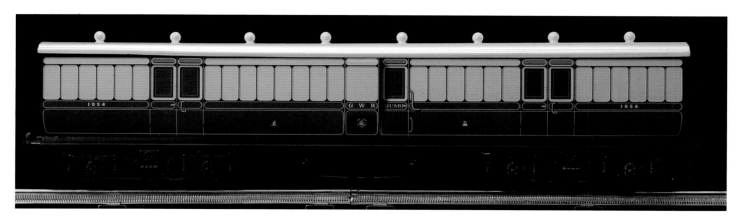

In fact, my reaction was more like, 'Are you totally insane?', as distinct from the borderline sanity we occupy during most of our ACE days. Despite my apprehension, I could not hold back the engineer in Andries. So off he went into the backwoods of Bangkok and put this highly unlikely project together. The result was AC/1 and the extension kit AC/1A. The ensuing bolt–together kit was to become acclaimed as gauge 0 masterpiece in the history of the hobby. Assembled like a super Meccano set with nuts and bolts, the resulting structure was unique. I should mention that Andries came from a very distinguished family of engineers and it is fitting that the generic shape of the canopy was inspired by a picture of a similar structure erected by the Dutch in Dedung Djati, Java before the turn of the Twentieth Century. So my initial reservations towards this project were unfounded. The AC/1 has found great success throughout the gauge 0 world. Six of these structures will be erected on the ACE Muhlkreis Junction layout in Austria of which more later.

By 2003, a detectable rhythm had established itself at ACE after the hectic and, at times, chaotic first eight years. Looking back on those years I have often reflected what a relatively quiet life I might have led after all the hurly-burly of publishing (13 Frankfurt Book Fairs, co-editions in America, France, Germany, Switzerland and Japan) and then running New Cavendish with Narisa, in tandem with The London Toy Museum, for nearly ten years . However, the calling to stake another claim as a toy and model train maker beckoned. My previous escapade with Bassett Lowke Railways in the late 1960s is covered in *The Bassett-Lowke Story,* a book I published during my New Cavendish days so I will not retread old ground here.

## THE ACE ALUMNI

I think at this point I should mention some of the people who in many cases, out of love for the subject, gave ACE the benefit of their knowledge and support. On the commercial front, Terry Barnicote of 'Much Ado About Toys' up in Stratford-upon-Avon was the first to see the commercial possibilities of retailing ACE to a wider audience than just members of the HRCA. Over the years, as the ACE line  developed, he enthusiastically supported us – some times a little too enthusiastically,  leaving me to fend off anxious would–be buyers who could not always understand why Much Ado's delivery announcements seem to be at odds with events on the ground. Alan Brown in the South came on board first as an advisor and then as a most enthusiastic dealer in all things ACE. He pioneered the sale of ACE products through an increasing number of enthusiast meetings and has always been on hand with his mythical hammer to knock any errant ACE equipment into shape. Through Alan's network, Mike Allen's calm influence was brought to bear on developing ACE production, particularly regarding wheel standards and electrical theory. John Mayo, a skilled clock maker and restorer, came to ACE in a similar way. John prepared the most perfect E/1 mechanism which required no lubrication at all. It is a prized possession in our archive. John Ovendon and Martin Wright were often on hand to man our far flung exhibition programmes. Dave Moss, apart from being an early convert to the ACE project, was instrumental in introducing me to Len Mills when he was developing the Corgi/Bassett-Lowke line. That introduction was later to have a significant influence on the development of ACE.

It was Alan Brown's introduction to Brian Wright (brother of Jeff Wright of Henley Meccano fame) that was to take ACE coach production to another level. As has been mentioned, my long association with John Cooper throughout the New Cavendish years had flowed into the early artwork required for the C/1 and C/2 series, together with the catalogue and advertising requirements. However the technology was advancing at such a pace that John as a freelance designer found himself unable to continue the investment in constantly changing technology and opted for a quieter life as a carpenter and gardener. After a long career with a major bank, Brian took early retirement and mastered the art of producing digital artwork for application as overlays on gauge 0 coach stock that required rejuvenation or a change of use and/or livery. From this introduction has flowed the artwork for all our coach series from C/4 onwards and now for our ACE/Wright Series, where ACE bodies are given totally new appearances via Brian's stunning overlays.

However, it is the artwork for our printed litho series where Brian's mastery of the medium (on a computer built by his son) which has led to the lithography on the C/4 Gresley Teak  range – unequalled in the reproduction of original teak by any of the great producers of the past. Not only is Brian a great artist in his field, but also for ACE an added bonus is his enormous repertoire of real railway practice knowledge.

## ONWARDS AND UPWARDS: C4 – C11

This brings the story to the most prolific period of production from 2003 onwards when the C/4 through to C/11 series of coaches were printed and gradually brought into production. A decision to produce a 40cm range of British coaches finally broke the link with the original specification that the C/1 and C/2 ranges should be able to pass on 2ft radius Hornby parallel curves.

Andries as referred to in Chapter 1 acquired the Darstaed range from Marcel Darphin and it was always his intention to bring back those items. His ambition was also to produce British-style Pullmans and this drawing depicted how these might look.

A Brighton Belle was another project dear to his heart. ACE events overtook this activity but in 2006 British Mark 1 Pullmans will be introduced in the ACE 40cm series.

ACE C/1 Nord sets were used in the construction of German Triebwagen sets, the first batch seen here under construction. A further batch using a Weinhold mechanism is in preparation. Jurgen Weinhold is the host of the Tuttlingen event.

81

It became a tradition that the rear cover of the Christmas edition of the HRCA Journal was devoted to a Christmas image albeit railway orientated one. Here are examples of several of these images.

ACE layout at Fortnum & Mason, Piccadilly, London - Christmas 2002

*A picture of the fabled ACE Fortnum and Mason layout that ran daily in the run up to Christmas 2002. This picture of an E/2 taken opposite the Royal Academy (left) is probably the only time a gauge 0 loco has functioned in a window in that street. It was in this window that Alan Brown dressed in green overalls like a garden gnome was, in a moment of contemplation while setting up the layout, mistaken for a window ornament by two American tourists. They were extremely alarmed when Alan sprang to life.*

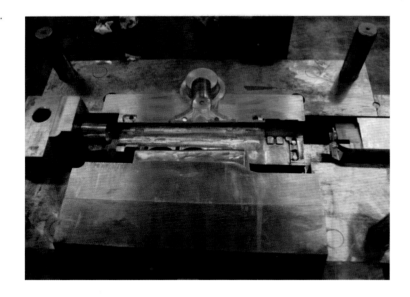

*The first test rig for the A4 chassis.*

To produce an 0 gauge Pacific body requires a large tool. It should be remembered that most cast bodies for kit produced gauge 0 models use rubber moulds that quickly deteriorate after relatively few castings in the low hundreds are spun off. The A4 and the A3, and the Castle Class to follow, utilise high pressure casting tools to give constant quality over long runs. This is a much more expensive process but differentiates between artisanal production which often employ pewter and those using industrial techniques which are true diecast.

85

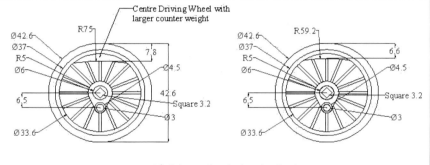

**060 Driving Wheels (16 Spokes)**

*The advent of email has made communications between far flung centres of operation much easier. Here an emailed picture of the E/5 0-6-0 first chassis mock up in brass, cast version and wheel drawings just to remind London that things were progressing. Some time later a running mock up was pictured on the ACE portable layout during the Tuttlingen 2005 meeting in Southern Germany.*

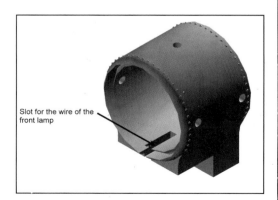

*Isometric software enables details such as this projection of the E/5 smoke box to be assessed prior to tool making.*

Little did I think that when I went on the 1969 Flying Scotsman Tour of the East Coast of the United States wearing my Bassett-Lowke Railways hat, that 37 years later I would be producing a gauge 0 A3 in competition with resurrected Bassett-Lowke now under the wing of Corgi Classics.

Alan Pegler, the then owner of Flying Scotsman will be endorsing our locomotive when it appears in late 2005. How wheels turn in life. Incidentally we will also be producing a version of 4472 as it ran in the USA. Also illustrated is the ACE A3 E5 with an ACE C/10 Tourist Stock Set.

Gresley's teak bow ended stock from the 1920s was chosen as it would enable trains such as 'Flying Scotsman' to be constituted in 7mm scale. The 35cm coach equated to 51ft in real practice, which happened to be the length of the shorter Gresley bow ended stock. However, the mainline stock was over 60 ft and this length would have ruled out parallel working over shorter Hornby radii. They were designated C/4 and have proved enormously popular. The first ACE articulated unit, namely the Gresley 1926 sleeping car set, was also produced and this system was to form the basis of the East Coast streamlined sets culminating in the seven car Silver Jubilee set C/11. Most of these sets are illustrated at the table of manufactured items at the end of the book

Running parallel with the C/4 range were the 35cm 'blood and custard' C/5 range. Hornby gauge 0 did not survive long enough to see a bogie version of these BR Mark 1 coaches. Bassett-Lowke, however, did produce a slightly shorter version of the Mark 1 in the post-war period. I have always thought that this series was somewhat dull and not enough effort went into making them more attractive. Needless to say, today they sell up to three times the price of the ACE equivalent. I do not think this situation will last too much longer when the C/5 series goes out of production.

## MOVING ONWARDS FROM 2005

The 2005 tin printing session included a new phase in ACE thinking, namely the production of a 40cm range in all the main BR Mark 1 regional sets. Added to those are a unique range of Mark 1 Pullmans. All these coaches will have as standard insulated wheel sets, thus broadening their appeal to both two-rail and three-rail enthusiasts. This printing also included a rake of five PLM cars, the company not covered in the C/1F series. The British range of 40cm 2/3 rail coaches are numbered C/12 to C/14. A table of the coaches in the series is included at the back of the book.

The freight sector was not overlooked and while the G/1 Tanker series had a very protracted development period, sets 1 – 6 of the petrol tanker sets came to the market in late 2004 followed by the G/1M Milk Tanker sets. Once again these very keenly priced vehicles made comparison with the often inflated prices of the Hornby and Bassett-Lowke originals look distinctly incongruous. Customer reaction to these lines was enthusiastic, proving that the generation of collectors who were in many cases happy to have static collections, were now warming to the idea of contemporary gauge 0 ready to run equipment. So ACE in its small way, has changed the historical course of this evergreen hobby. None of this denies that or-

ganisations like the HRCA (for many years guided by its Chairman, John Kitchen) and latterly The Bassett-Lowke Society, as well as the Train Collectors Society, have actively encouraged running sessions of their chosen makes . The absence of anything new was beginning to deny this pool of enthusiasm the oxygen of novelty. Enter ACE Trains and later Corgi/Bassett-Lowke. As with so many things, American three-rail devotees have for many years been served with tidal waves of new product and running had become subject to mind boggling, technological advances – a far cry from the original clatter and bang of simple tinplate railroads. That is a separate discourse and suffice to say, ACE products in all their relative simplicity have been warmly received by the US Hobby press and its expanding list of customers.

At this point of its development, ACE is poised to bring out an ex-LNER A3 Pacific, a series of 0-6-0 tender locomotives and an ex GWR Castle Class locomotive. Both Collett and Hawksworth 40 cm coaches have been printed and pressed and a range of goods rolling stock including vans, wagons and a brake van. Future plans will feature a 'Warship' diesel locomotive and the LMS Coronation trains plus a Southern Railway Pacific locomotive, again using high pressure die casting for the main body shells.

Finally, a brief word on two important ACE developments, the most important of which occurred in the spring of 2005 when we formed an association with Len Mills following his untimely departure from the Corgi/Bassett-Lowke enterprise. While this ACE history is not primarily concerned with other companies policy decisions, it seems inconceivable to us that Len was not vital to any onward development of the new Bassett-Lowke project. Len has now established a distribution centre for ACE at Enderby, near Leicester, together with a maintenance and repair business for several makes including ACE and non warranty work for Bassett-Lowke. He will also pay visits to Bangkok and act as consultant on existing and upcoming projects.

A further development will be the construction of an extremely large three-rail layout in Austria to be known as The 'Muhlkreis Junction' Railway. The track will be supplied by The Maldon Rail Centre and will include tinplate buildings, no less than six AC/1 Canopies together with a collection of buildings from the late Dennis Jenkinson's finescale layout and an extensive Elastolin Zoo. Details of this will appear in future Newsletters, and we hope that visitors will be able to visit the layout in upper Austria in the near future. The layout will also display the extremely rare Marklin double bridge of 1919. All this is a far cry from those long lost days when a simple circle of track beckoned so many into the magical world of gauge 0 trains.

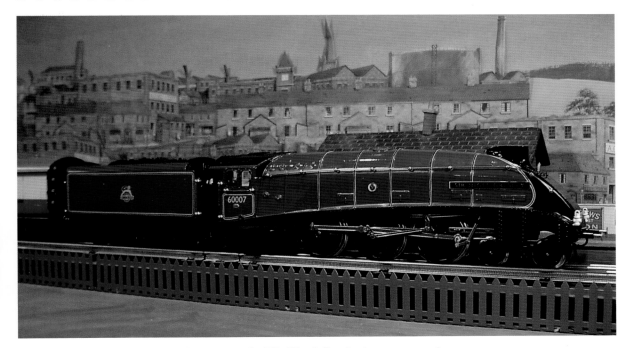

*A further example of a special run, namely 'Sir Nigel Gresley' as preserved made for The A4 Society, here seen on the Ladbroke Grove test track.*

At an event held at The Brighton Toy and Model Museum (founded by Chris Littledale renowned toy restorer and lifelong railway enthusiast) an ACE A4 drawn up alongside a 1938 vintage Bassett Lowke example. The latter was the only 'commercial' offering of this Pacific by any other of the major train makers and was way beyond the means of all but the most well off model railway operator. The phenomenon of static toy and model collecting as against running was virtually unheard of in the pre-war period.

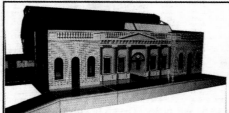

*BRM advert signals things to come. Synchronising advertising and delivery at ACE has always been a problem. That eventually virtually everything flagged up arrives does not always lessen the justified frustration of our ever growing volume of eager customers. Unlike some of our rivals we can never be accused of flooding the market.*

# ACE TRAINS A4 IS HERE

*Mike Ennis has the latest news on this new O gauge model*

The first photograph of the new Gresley A4 from Ace Trains running on a large display layout at London Department store, Fortnum and Mason, is seen here. Two pre-production models of the famous pre-war LNER streamlined locomotive in Garter blue livery created an impressive sight hauling trains of eight of the new LNER teak coaches, also made by Ace Trains, although numbers and nameplates had not been added.

The locomotives, together with other ACE Trains and further A4s as they begin to be delivered, will be running on the display until Christmas Eve at the famous London store in Piccadilly. The layout is on the fourth floor as part of the 'Once Upon a Time' Christmas feature, the largest display of 16th to early 20th century toys, dolls, teddy bears, trains, mechanica and automata on sale in Great Britain.

The Ace Trains layout, part of the 'Once upon a Time' display at Fortnum & Mason. *Mike Ennis*

## TOY TRAIN COLLECTORS BOOK

David Pressland, Pierce Carlson, Narisa Chakra (editor), Paul Klein Schiphorst (author) and Allen Levy at the offices of Ace Trains for the launch of *The Golden Years of Tin Toy Trains (1850-1909)*. *Mike Ennis*

The latest book published by New Cavendish Books will be of interest to train collectors. *The Golden Years of Tin Toy Trains (1850-1909)* by Paul Klein Schiphorst was launched at a party hosted at the offices of Ace Trains in London. The full colour 360 page 240mm x 300mm hardback book, complete with slipcase, is illustrated with more than 1,000 pictures. Featured are not only the trains of the period but also many of the rarely seen accessories from tunnels and public toilets to refreshment trolleys! Originally based on Paul Klein Schiphorst's own collection the book includes many unique and valuable items from the foremost tin toy collection in the world

including material which does not appear in catalogues or has never been photographed before.

A Märklin Midland Railway cart, one of the many delightful pictures in *The Golden Years of Tin Toy Trains' (1850-1909)*. Mike Ennis

*The confluence of two projects, namely the launching of the last great Toy Train book by New Cavendish and ACE activity in 2004.*

*The nature of the model railway business today is the prevalence of numerous shows at which both the trade and private individuals display and run their equipment. One such regular event is the quarterly meeting at Sandown Park. Above, part of the ACE stand in 2005 with Mike Allen, a long term 'guru' of ACE, lurking in the background. Other pictures show all hands on deck when the need arises.*

## ACE IN FOREIGN FIELDS.

*A series 1 A4 alongside a reproduction of a 'Marklin Cock O' the North' in 2003. A series 2 BR liveried ACE A4 shows it paces with an ACE tanker trains in 2004 and a train of ACE tankers awaits motive power in a generous siding. 'Mallard' roars away with a C/7 Coronation set on the ACE layout in Tuttlingen 2005. Several other pictures illustrate the wide variety of models on roster. Of particular note is the Prussian 4-4-4 heading a train of ACE C/1 Germanised Nord coaches. Right – 'Sir Nigel Gresley' on the Brandywine public display layout in Pennsylvania USA.*

*An introduction of ACE Petrol Tankers to Europe for the first time.*

SIR NIGEL STOPS FOR WATER    KIBRI    LIONEL    AF "CHICAGO"
AMERICAN FLYER (BING)    SIGNAL    PEDISTAL    WATER TOWER
WATER TOWER    BRIDGE    CRANE

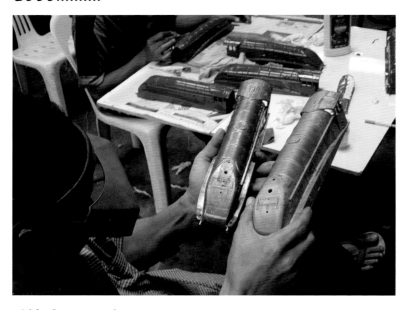

*A4 body preparation.*

*Backhead inspired by earlier
FS Elettren Pacific.*

*Above: The first working mock up on trial on John
Ovendon's loft railway in Hampshire.*

*Right: Also illustrated is an alloy shell mock-up to
obtain initial measurement information prior to the die
casting tool being made.*

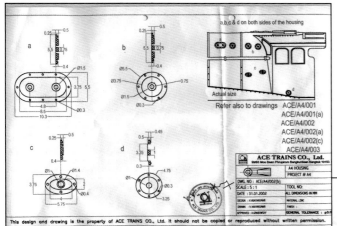

a,b,c & d on both sides of the housing

Actual size
Refer also to drawings
ACE/A4/001
ACE/A4/001(a)
ACE/A4/002
ACE/A4/002(a)
ACE/A4/002(c)
ACE/A4/003

ACE TRAINS CO., Ltd.
99/93 Moo Baan Phuptorn Bangkunthien Bangkok 10150.

| | |
|---|---|
| DWG. NO : ACE/A4/002(b) | A4 HOUSING |
| | PROJECT # A4 |
| SCALE : 5 : 1 | TOOL NO: |
| DATE : 31.01.2002 | ALL DIMENSIONS IN MM |
| DESIGN : V.VIJAYKUMAR | MATERIAL : ZINC |
| DRAWN : V.VIJAYKUMAR | FINISH : |
| APPROVED : A.GRABOWSKY | GENERAL TOLERANCE : ±0.0 |

This design and drawing is the property of ACE TRAINS CO., Ltd. It should not be copied or reproduced without written permission.

*Various aspects of the development of the E/4 from drawings to body finishing. A further B17 variation was considered but the A4 casting could not be shortened. Two later samples would run for three months at Fortnum and Mason which led to some early modifications.*

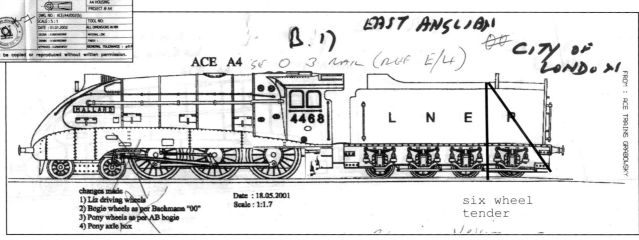

ACE A4    SG O 3 RAIL (REF E/4)

B.17    EAST ANGLIAN    CITY OF LONDON

4468    L N E R

FROM : ACE TRAINS GRABOWSKY

changes made
1) Liz driving wheels
2) Bogie wheels as per Bachmann "00"
3) Pony wheels as per AB bogie
4) Pony axle box

Date : 18.05.2001
Scale : 1:1.7

six wheel tender

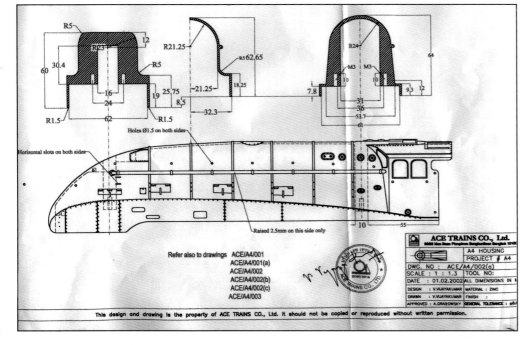

Refer also to drawings    ACE/A4/001
ACE/A4/001(a)
ACE/A4/002
ACE/A4/002(b)
ACE/A4/002(c)
ACE/A4/003

Holes Ø1.5 on both sides

Horizontal slots on both sides

Raised 2.5mm on this side only

ACE TRAINS CO., Ltd.
99/93 Moo Baan Phuptorn Bangkunthien Bangkok 1016C

| | |
|---|---|
| | A4 HOUSING |
| | PROJECT # A4 |
| DWG. NO : ACE/A4/002(a) | |
| SCALE : 1 : 1.3 | TOOL NO: |
| DATE : 01.02.2002 | ALL DIMENSIONS IN M |
| DESIGN : V.VIJAYAKUMAR | MATERIAL : ZINC |
| DRAWN : V.VIJAYAKUMAR | FINISH : |
| APPROVED : A.GRABOWSKY | GENERAL TOLERANCE : ±0. |

This design and drawing is the property of ACE TRAINS CO., Ltd. It should not be copied or reproduced without written permission.

*Assembly of A4 handrails in Bangkok.*

95

*The Wrights in Bangkok, 2004.*
*From right to left: Brian Wright, Andries and*
*Michelle Grabowsky, Margaret Wright.*

*Andries Grabowsky admires his handy work at Tuttlingen, 2005. Crating a minor masterpiece across half the globe is a distinct challenge. Through all our efforts the numerous problems of creating this model have been overcome. From a relatively simple four coupled mechanism of the E/1 series to this sleek and powerful Pacific was for the ACE team a quantum leap.*

*Conference at the Bangkok factory attended by*
*Vijay, Andries and Brian.*

John Shawe and Len Mills discuss the ongoing project for a high pressure live steam version of the A4. One of the surviving 'Fortnum and Mason' Pacifics can be seen on the shelf which will be converted by John as a running test bed to consider the feasibility of the project.

Len and Andries discuss the finer points of the A3 casting along with discussions concerning E/5 production. The meeting was at Strasbourg on the way back from Tuttlingen 2005, before Andries headed off to family in Holland and Len and I returned to the UK.

Two generations of Ravasinis, the Elettren family pose with Andries
at Tuttlingen, 2004 – the great annual gathering of all contemporary
three-rail personalities and products.

Nuova
# ELETTREN s.n.c.

Maurizio Ravasini

Via A. D'Intimiano, 7
**20025 LEGNANO** (MI) - Italia
Tel. e Fax (0331) 546.597

*An unlikely winner. When the wartime version of the A4 was
first mooted we thought sales would be minimal. Enthusiasm
for this type exceeded all expectations and whereas the final
production was small, many more could have been produced.
Here, two examples on a customer's layout stand alongside
another masterpiece, the Bassett-Lowke tinplate A3 of the
1950s.
Photo by Keith Munday.*

The Elettren Pacific, was the inspiration for the ACE
A4(E/4) Bruce Coleman a great friend of ACE and serious
model railway Francophile can be seen in the background.

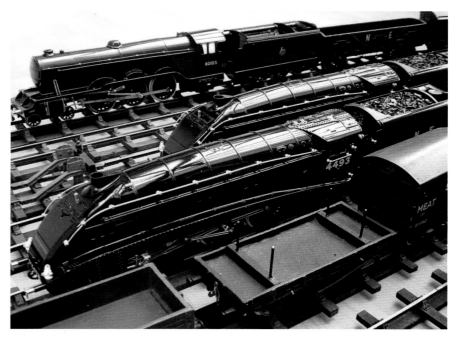

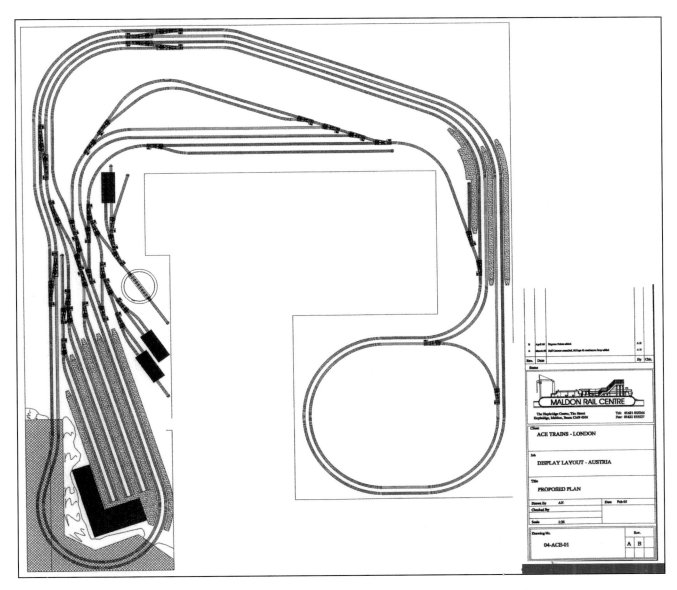

*The layout at Muhlkreis Junction that will include a six Canopy ACE terminus. Track as drawn up and supplied by the Malden Rail Centre. The overall measurements of the layout being 8m x 9.2m (26ft x 30ft). The two main running tracks each measure 50 meters (164ft) in length.*

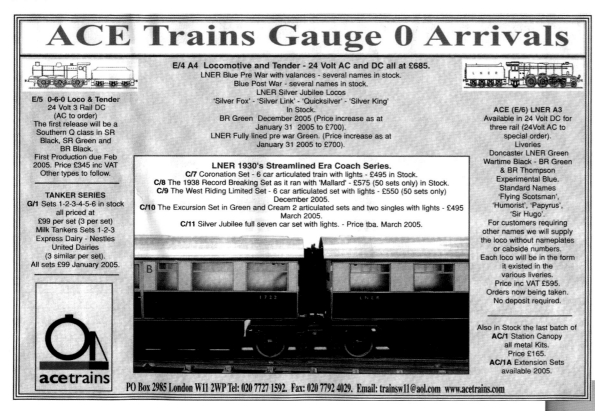
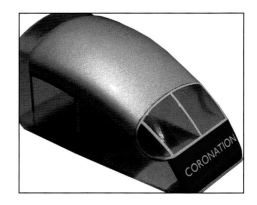
*ACE launched its LNER inter-war East Coast special coach set programme several years ago. The programme was completed in 2005 and comprised sets C/7 through to C/12. These sets depicted art deco of the 1930s and the love affair with speed cut short by WW II. Illustrated here, an advertisement announcing the progress of the series a contemporary shot of The Coronation headed by A4 'Dominion of Canada', part of a rake of the C/7 set taken in New Zealand by our forthright friend John Agnew and the rear end component of the legendary 'Beaver Tail' summer car, issued in 2005.*

*The 'Beaver Tail' as rebuilt after WW2.*

*As a thank you for all the encouragement given to our daughter Emily at Trevor Roberts School, I presented the school with this narrow gauge Accucast steam loco to run on the school playground layout. Naturally it was named Emily. To complete the extended family connection, I include a picture of Dominic Chakra Thomson (Narisa's son and Hugo's half-brother) filling her up during the first day of running.*

101

**Out of the Box**

**Onto the track**

**Years of reliability**

**ACE**

*An ad in 2004 HRCA Journal espousing simple virtues.*

*Horst Reichert, who for many years operated a toy restoration business just off Queensway in West London, before returning to the Black Forest in his native Germany to set up his line of reproduction trains and Marklin style stations and accessories. Here seen greeting his co-manufacturer, Andries Grabowsky at Tuttlingen, 2005. In 2003, Horst was running original gauge 4 live steam Schoenner and Bing at Tuttlingen. The world of trains brings together some extremely original characters.*

*One of the great pleasures of visiting Japan in 2004 was our trip to Karasawa, home of the Bandai Toy Corporations World Toy Museum. This museum contains (virtually intact) the collection that I built up at The London Toy and Model Museum. It was a double pleasure to see old 'friends' so well presented and cared for. We took the opportunity to present the museum with and ACE A4 to stand alongside the museum's Bassett-Lowke example. A rare poster of an earlier project in Japan, following the London Toy Museum's major touring exhibition in Australia. Once again, a small organisation with big ideas turned to reality quickly.*

*Seeing product for the first time never palls. Here, Andries presents the*
*first Petrol Tankers at Ladbroke Grove. A glass of wine is never far away*
*when Andries is in town. Later the G/1 Milk Tankers appeared.*

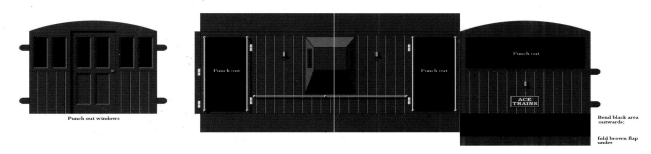

Punch out windows

Punch out

Bend black area
outwards;

fold brown flap
under

*Tin origami that will fold into the new ACE Brake Van and other
goods wagons etc, which, together with our Petrol and Milk Tanker
series, will evolve into a significant wagon and van programme.*

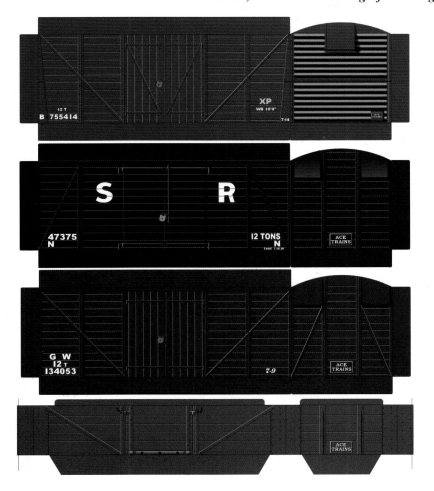

*While on a family trip to Japan in 2004, we took the opportunity
to visit the Aster factory at Yokohama. Here, the two leading lights
of that extraordinary firm Toyoki Inoue and Satoshi Sasaki which
changed the face of gauge 1 kit and ready-to-run locomotives.*

*This was the final configuration chosen for the E/5 0-6-0 locomotive.*

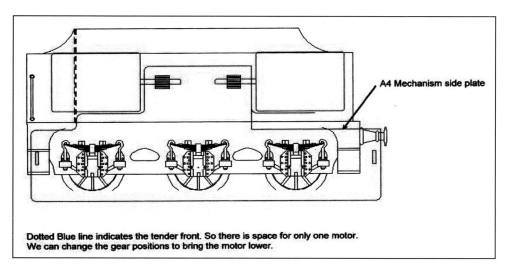

A4 Mechanism side plate

Dotted Blue line indicates the tender front. So there is space for only one motor.
We can change the gear positions to bring the motor lower.

*These two motor arrangements for the E/5 never gained the approval of the board of gurus but nonetheless showed originality. Likewise the command and control prototype (top), relying on a constant 18 volts on the track proved to be an expensive non-starter.*

ACE presented a unique BR A4 named 'Terence Cuneo' to raise funds via auction for the sculpture that was eventually erected at Waterloo. This was a particular pleasure to me as I had known Terry for many years and had the privilege of publishing the majority of his significant books. Here I am seen presenting the loco to Carol Cuneo, now the proud owner.

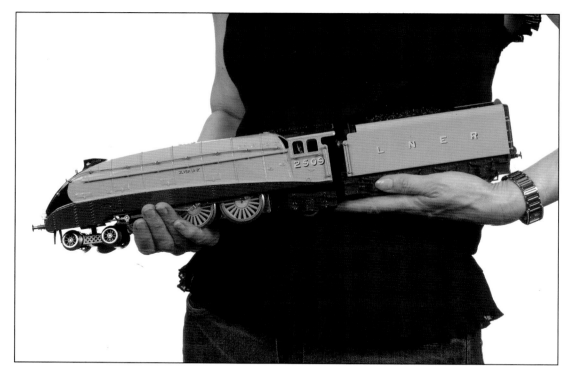

*Size matters – gauge 0 can be run in surprisingly small spaces and I defy anyone to explain the logic of running 00 in a garden despite the booklets put out to explain the techniques. N and 00 if you like scenery and a fixed layout gauge 0 coarse scale layout if you want to play and both hear and see your trains. This wonderful shot of an ACE BR A4 with a rake of C/5 coaches emphasises this point.*

*Various ACE mechanisms over the years. All had had all gear driven axles in common. We avoided the more common and cheaper worm drive system as this does not always enable the motor to read its direction. Also illustrated is the manual AC reverse switching arrangement which, together with DC and neutral positions, were first introduced in the EMU series. A similar arrangement was carried through to the E/2 in DC only. In future, all motive power will be 24DC with AC as an option.*

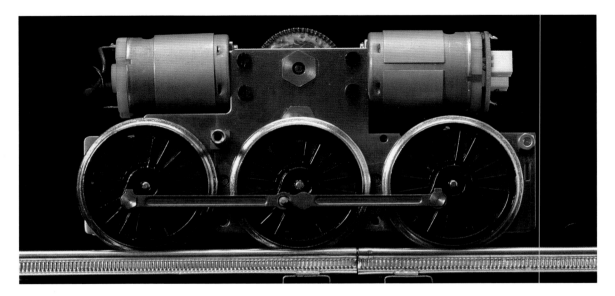

The Train Room at Ladbroke Grove has been transformed from a general collection of post London Toy Museum items (once a collector....) to a test track and archive room for ACE. Also illustrated, high speed action on the multi-level test tracks. In the near future all the archive material will move out of London to a new ACE Museum in Leicester. This Museum I hope will be small but almost perfect.

---

## Great destination

### Ace's O gauge station canopy

FINALLY, ALL OF THOSE grand, O gauge passenger trains have an equally grand destination: Ace Trains station canopy.

Ace Trains is a British company that makes tinplate reproductions of classic Hornby-style O gauge locomotives and rolling stock. Ace's station canopy kit, distributed in the United States by Weaver Models, is its first structure.

And what a structure it is. The tinplate-style canopy is 24 inches long, a shade under 12 inches high, and, depending on how you configure the platforms, 14⅛ to 16⅛ inches wide. The openings on each end are 5⅝ inches tall from ground level to the bottom edge of the half-circle windows. The canopy weighs a hefty 18 pounds.

With the adjustable platforms moved to their widest position, there is enough room for three O gauge tracks inside the canopy. Fourth and fifth tracks can be placed along the two outer edges of the canopy beneath the awnings.

All the arched and straight girders are made from nickel-plated, die-cast metal. The platforms, gabled roof, and awnings are lithographed sheet metal. The windows are made of a Plexiglas-like material. Black printing divides each of the 14 window sections into smaller panes.

It took me three evenings to assemble the canopy. The legs and arched girders are held together with metric-

size machine screws and nuts. The platforms, sheet-metal roofs, and smaller girders that hold the window panels in place are assembled with self-tapping machine screws. In all, the kit uses 84 slot-head screws, enough to make you appreciate the invention of the Phillips-head screw. (Phillips-head screws, however, would be an anachronism for a prewar-style train or structure.)

A few of the self-tapping screws were a struggle to thread, and a 5.5-millimeter wrench was a big help tightening the nuts that hold the main girders together. Also, one of the awnings bowed slightly when I lined up all of its mounting holes.

It took me a few minutes to understand how the platforms with their elongated mounting holes are adjusted inward and outward on the eight legs of the main arches. The left and right

platforms are interchangeable, allowing you to position the platforms about 2 inches in or out from the center of the structure, depending on your layout needs. Small ovals of sheet metal that look like floor drains are used to fill the gaps in the elongated platform holes.

All the parts are clearly marked, and there are extra screws and nuts of each size in case you lose one on the floor. Ace provides a multi-page instruction booklet with numerous diagrams and a full parts list. While this is not a difficult kit to assemble, past experience building things like bicycles, metal utility shelves, and Erector sets is helpful.

The canopy kit also comes with two stairwells for the imaginary tunnel connecting the two platforms, two 12-inch lithographed platform extensions, and two 8-inch ramps.

Since the Ace canopy is a kit, it does

Continued on page 98

---

*As a result of attending the giant train meeting at York in the USA, a limited distribution was set up with Weaver Models. A batch of A4's had been darkened slightly for reasons unknown. They were all named 'Golden Eagle' and sold with a Coronation Set on an exclusive basis to Weaver. The price was considerably discounted but this deal proved that borders do not exist in the global market place. Whereas the deal was exclusive to the USA, various sets were split up and sold outside the exclusive territory. ACE would be unlikely to repeat this arrangement and all sales to the USA are to direct customers only.*

111

## Blood & Custard

Ace Trains' O gauge British Railways Mk. I coach set

UNTIL RECENT YEARS, enthusiasts of British three-rail O gauge trains were the hobby equivalents of Maytag repairmen – pretty lonely blokes.

In 1997, Ace Trains took the first steps to revitalize the British three-rail tinplate market with a line of locomotives and rolling stock. Ace equipment has been produced in the classic Hornby prewar style, but with modern production quality. Most recently, Ace has released a nice set of lithographed British Railways Mk. I "Corridor" cars.

Corridor cars are simply cars with a corridor, or hallway, running the length of the car. While that's the norm in North America, older European cars are often broken up into cabins, accessed only through exterior doors. The British Railways standard or Mk. I cars were first produced in 1951.

The cars featured a strong steel underframe and steel pillars at each end. They were constructed in a wide range of types, including 1st and 2nd classes, side corridor and open coaches, and sleepers and dining cars. For many years they formed the core of the United Kingdom's passenger car fleet.

The Ace cars, which are similar to Hornby O gauge cars, are offered in the red-and-yellow scheme that British railfans dub "blood and custard." Their metal shells offer terrific lithography, capturing as good, if not better detail than original lithographed cars. The Ace cars have nice simulated diaphragms, and they come with removable nameplates for the train *The Elizabethan*.

The four-wheel trucks are die-cast metal with metal wheels, and the lithographed body shell rides on a sheet-metal frame. The average weight of the cars is 1 pound, 11 ounces each. The couplers are of the British link-type, and the buffers are sprung. The brake van (the trailing car) has an illuminated lantern out back picking up power from two large, spoon-type sliding shoes.

British outline, three-rail trains aren't

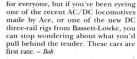

for everyone, but if you've been eyeing one of the recent AC/DC locomotives made by Ace, or one of the new DC three-rail rigs from Bassett-Lowke, you can stop wondering about what you'd pull behind the tender. These cars are first rate. – *Bob*

---

**O GAUGE BRITISH RAILWAYS MK. I COACH SET BY ACE TRAINS**

**Price:** £215 (approximately $360 depending on the exchange rate)

**Features:** Die-cast metal trucks, prewar style sheet metal construction, lithographed metal shell, link couplers, illuminated end-of-train lantern

**Pros:** Superb lithography

**Cons:** Limited distribution, no interior decoration or illumination

Made in Thailand for Ace Trains

Available through Ace Trains at acetrains.com, Railmaster Exports, 29 Pupuke Rd., Birkenhead, Auckland 1310, New Zealand, order online at www.railmaster.co.nz, or Britannia Models, Box 45015, Surrey, British Columbia, Canada V4A 7R8, check out britanniamodels.com or call 604-538-2698.

*Various reviews of ACE products contained in Classic Toy Trains. Although not a major market, the American enthusiasm for originality and quality beams out of these appraisals.*

---

*Below is part of a review of the A4 entitled 'Duke of Diecast'.*

CONTINUED FROM PAGE 83

  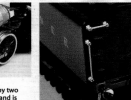

The Ace A4 is sleek, powered by two can-style motors, looks great, and is made to run, not just sit on a shelf!

and rear drivers. All three axles are geared, and all of the driver wheels are flanged. The drive mechanism is designed with enough swing to negotiate relatively tight 42-inch-diameter curves without the need for flange-less center drivers. There are no traction tires.

Ace locomotives are designed for AC and DC operation. A rod on the front of the tender is connected to an internal slide switch. Pull it one way for AC and the other for DC. Power pickup is through two sliding shoes on the bottom of the tender. Another rod is used to reverse the locomotive's direction when operating with AC power.

An electrical tether connects the locomotive and tender. The female end of the tether is affixed to a small plastic block just beneath the front edge of the tender frame. Ours was broken during shipping, so the tether end hung freely instead of being held fast to the frame.

This turned out to be a blessing in disguise. Why? Because of the BBF factor (Bob's Big Fingers).

You need nimble fingers to connect the two ends of the electrical tether and the metal drawbar connecting the locomotive and tender. My fingers are a bit

too large for the job. But, unintentionally, the broken plastic block made the female end of the tether much easier to grasp. Go figure.

The decoration of the locomotive was first-rate, and application of numbers and the *Mallard* nameplate and commemorative plaque gives the model a special look. The paint is smooth as silk, and, as the photos show, it has a high gloss.

Five different passenger coach sets, including the *Coronation* and record breaking sets are available from Ace.

### On the test track

Ace's A4 locomotive is conventional-control mode only. Our sample *Mallard* is a smooth-running locomotive, and it is very responsive to changes in speed.

The low-speed average for our sample *Mallard* was 15 scale mph, while the high-speed average was 94 scale mph.

Drawbar pull for the 7-pound, 9-ounce locomotive was 1 pound. The train was easily capable of pulling a string of Ace passenger cars with a few Ace tank wagons coupled on the end. Just keep in mind that in the real world A4s weren't used for pulling 100-car coal trains.

The locomotive ran fine on O-54 and

O-72 diameter curves, although it was a snug fit on O-42 curves. On the O-42 Ross Custom track switches on one of our home test layouts, the pilot truck sometimes derailed when following the diverging route. The A4 is a large locomotive, and it is more at home on larger curves. It operated equally well on tubular track and on Atlas O and MTH solid-rail track.

While this locomotive does not have a sound system or even a whistle, the mechanical sounds it makes are a pleasure for any traditional operator. The bathtub shape of the shell increases the motor and drive-train noises, giving the *Mallard* quite a bit of personality.

I really love running the *Mallard*. It is as distinctive a locomotive as you'll find, and it delivered a very pleasing performance. If you're a fan of ultra-streamlined locomotives like the Dreyfuss Hudson or the Pennsy Torpedo, you'll want to check out the Ace A4. – *Bob Keller*

---

**O GAUGE LNER A4-CLASS PACIFIC 4-6-2 BY ACE TRAINS**

**Price:** $1,000 (depending on exchange rate)

**Features:** O-48 operation, die-cast metal construction, two can-style motors, illuminated marker lights, firebox glow, link couplers

**Pros:** Good-looking, solid performance, unique and attractive design

**Cons:** Limited distribution, and oh, that exchange rate!

Made in Thailand by Ace Trains

Available from Ace Trains at acetrains.com (North American orders pay no VAT); Railmaster Exports, at railmaster.co.nz; or Britannia Models, britanniamodels.com. For U.S. trade sales contact Weaver Models, 570-473-9434.

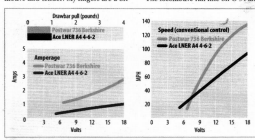

*Works drawing of proposed E/3 2-6-2 Tank locomotive,*
*postponed to enable work to proceed with the A4 (E5) project.*

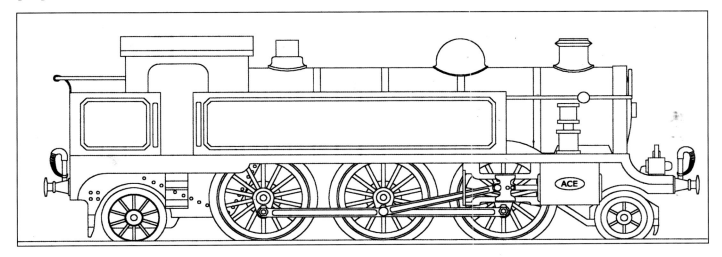

*The first of the Bangkok printed coaches, namely the C/4 and C/5 ranges,*
*were introduced as announced in this Railway Modeller advert.*

*Some alternative facade sketches by my son Hugo.*

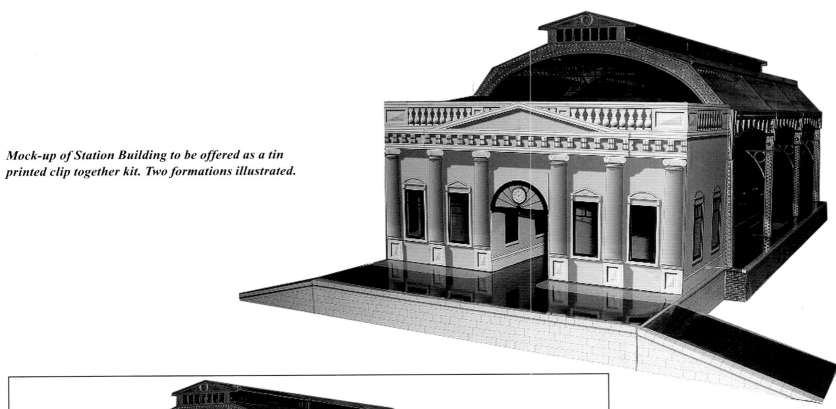

*Mock-up of Station Building to be offered as a tin printed clip together kit. Two formations illustrated.*

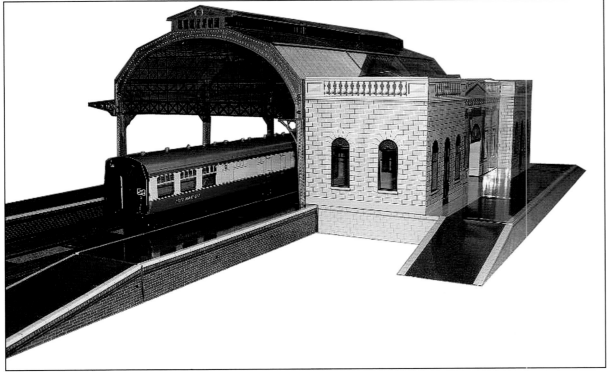

*This could almost be a wish list shot from a 1938 Hornby Dublo catalogue. It is, in fact, current ACE gauge 0, namely 'The Silver Jubilee' and 'Coronation' trains.*

*Two more offerings of A4s and their trains. Top with a Tourist Set C/10 below in their final BR form together with a C/5A set depicting BR Mark 1 'blood and custard' coaches.*

American gauge 0 is offered in 1/48 scale. This is illustrated in this front end confrontation between a Sunset Models Mercury Pacific and the ACE A4. The former should tower above the latter.

New observation car, a pre-production mock up of the beaver tail Summar Car for running with the ACE Coronation set.

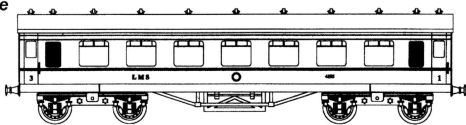

*An advert for the C/3 LMS kit range that hardly required advertising. At £35 per set complete with chopsticks for bending tabs, the consignment flew away. The roof had been modified to meet with the requirements of the upcoming C/5 series of BR Mark 1 coaches.*

## The Locomotive

The A1 class was envisaged by Edward Thompson in his standardisation plans for North East Region locomotives after nationalisation. None were built during his term in office apart from the rebuild of Gresley's original GNR Pacific No 4470 *Great Northern* which was given the sole classification A1/1. Thompson's original design was taken forward by his successor A. H. Peppercorn and the first A1 entered service in August 1948, named *W. P. Allen*.

Of the total complement of 49 engines, 20 were built at Doncaster and 29 at Darlington. The last locomotive of the batch entered service in 1949 and the last of the class, No 60145 *Saint Mungo*, was scrapped in 1966. The A1 first appeared at Kings Cross on 18th August 1948 and headed the inaugural run of the Tees-Tyne Pullman. The locomotives were allocated throughout the North and North East at Grantham, Copley Hill, Ardsley, York, Gateshead, Heaton, Haymarket and Polmadie. Despite some rough riding characteristics, during their fifteen years of active service they ran the highest annual mileages of all the Doncaster-built Pacifics and were the least troublesome. Five of the class were fitted with roller bearings, these being the lightest on maintenance.

J. F. Harrison, in his Presidential Address to the Institution of Locomotive Engineers in 1961, stated the A1 was the kind of locomotive Sir Nigel Gresley would have designed had he been alive.

## Some Technical Data

| | |
|---|---|
| Cylinders | 3 |
| Motion | Walschaerts |
| Boiler | Heating Surface including superheater 3141.04 sq.ft. |
| Boiler Pressure | 250 lb per sq ft. |
| Driving Wheels | 6ft 8ins. |
| Tractive effort | 85% 37,397 lb. |
| Length over buffers | 72ft 11¾in. |
| Weight: Loco and Tender full | 166 tons 11 cwts. |
| Max Axle Load | 22 tons 7 cwts. |
| Water Capacity | 5000 gallons. |
| Coal Capacity | 9 tons |

## The A1 Locomotive
### Project No 60163 TORNADO

*Let's make an A1!*

After decades of astonishing work in the field of steam locomotive preservation the A1 Locomotive Project aims to take the movement one step further with the construction of an entirely new main line locomotive – the 50th of the A1 Class – No 60163 – to be named *Tornado*.

All 49 of its predecessors were scrapped after dieselisation in the 1960's.

Read this leaflet and see how *you* can help this fabulous project to succeed.

*New Cavendish Books donated this fund raising brochure for the A1 project. Initially the locomotive was to be named New Cavendish in return for a substantial donation to the eventual Trust. However, pending certain legal formalities it became apparent that the project would need considerably more funding than originally thought. To this end I suggested that the name be a more universal one in terms of further fund raising. Despite other long scrapped locos having borne this name I suggested Tornado with its association with The RAF would be a more appropriate choice. The then managing committee agreed and although the project was to overrun its completion date and initial budget by a considerable margin the decision was the right one.*

*Alan Brown (right) laying tracks on the boardroom table at Bankers NM Rothschild. The event was the presentation of an E/2 train set to a long serving employee who was involved with the Railtrack flotation. Nothing to do with us, Guv!!*

*The New Team, Len and 'Dingle' Mills meet up with the old team at the Bassett-Lowke Society meeting at Mytchett 2005.*

*Glazing and assembly being applied to the C/4 series coaches at the Bangkok factory.*

| |
|---|
| (THE FLYING SCOTSMAN) KINGS CROSS - EDINBURGH |
| THE SCARBOROUGH FLYER |
| LONDON (EUSTON) - GLASGOW (CENTRAL) |
| THE MERSEYSIDE EXPRESS - LONDON (EUSTON) - LIVERPOOL (LIME SREET) |
| THE YORKSHIREMAN - LONDON (ST PANCRAS) - BRADFORD (EXCHANGE) |
| THE MANCUNIAN - LONDON (EUSTON) - MANCHESTER (LONDON ROAD) |
| OCEAN LINER EXPRESS - WATERLOO - SOUTHAMPTON DOCKS |
| KINGS CROSS - EDINBURGH - ABERDEEN |
| THE ROYAL SCOT |
| THE GOLDEN ARROW |
| THE BOURNEMOUTH BELLE |
| CORNISH RIVIERA LIMITED |
| TORBAY EXPRESS |
| QUEEN OF SCOTS |
| WATERLOO - SALISBURY AND EXETER |
| THE YORKSHIRE PULLMAN |
| THE BRISTOLIAN |
| CHELTENHAM SPA EXPRESS |
| LONDON, FOLKESTONE, DOVER, DEAL |
| THE ATLANTIC COAST EXPRESS |

*Coach boards for existing trains and future trains.*

121

ACE participated in a major exhibition organised by The Bassett-Lowke Society at the National Railway Museum in York. Here, Len Mills casts his spell over various ACE sets.

Simon Goodyear, the popular and timeless (he rarely seems to be aware of time) proprietor of Train Time, observes the joint stand at York.

The Editor
Lowko News
George Lane
Stanton
Nr. Bury St. Edmunds, Suffolk IP3        August 27 2003

Dear Bob

Can I pick up on Alan Cliff's letter in the Autumn Newsletter. 'The Future of our Hobby' which commented on David Bowers earlier correspndence.

The quick answer of course is that nobody knows.

Had new products not come along the answer may well have been more emphatic namely that the cost of entry kept the next generation (lets say the 40 year olds upwards) out of contention. Running very expensive vintage trains would not be attractive particularly for people who had no youthful memories of them.

However that is not  the case and hard as it is to comprehend more varied ready to run gauge 0  rolling stock in particular is available than in the past.

Wearing my ACE hat we have made printed tinplate Caledonian and  London Brighton and South Coast  Stock which apart from some quaint and very rare Hornby four wheelers  were never available from any of the pre war companies including their German sub contractors.

All those and versions of non corridor GWR, LNER , Southern LMS,LNWR and BR coaches plus main line Gresley Bow ended teaks and BR Mark 1 Blood and Custards ( with due apologies to BL rather restrained version and Exleys very expensive versions)) have rejuvenated the market in ready to run Gauge 0 coarse scale. These at prices that are generally accepted as being very reasonable.. All this and two EMU sets namely the ACE Met and Southern EMU's. Our LMS set is of course not unique but was ( its sold out) at least £1000 cheaper than its illustrious forebear.

Bassett Lowke /Corgi have also joined the party so for to days beginner there is a relative wealth of 'new start' material.

Nothing is for certain of course but 00 and HO eventually gives way to Gauge 0 as whereas the original 00 material was aimed at the young those boys become old chaps and cannot see those fiddly little trains as the years go by. I think the hobby has been given a new lease of life so *nil desperandum*.

Yours truly,
Allen Levy ( Hon BLS).

*Thoughts on the way ahead.*

*The team of Mills and Brown spent a week at St Ulrich in October 2005 erecting the first two circuits of the Mulkreis Junction Railway. Here shown is the first train to complete the circuit. The train comprises an ACE E4 and C/12 followed by a doubled up Pola Maxi German coach, a rare Arnholt Austrian Coach bearing the destination Linz followed by a gas container truck still bearing its price tag '1 bier'. Very mixed traffic. Getting these circuits running was a tribute to the electrical simplicity of three-rail opera-tion. The next phase of this railway will be completed in Spring 2006 after the snows have gone.*

*A4(E/4) in foreground awaits the whistle before setting off with 'The Silver Jubilee' (C/11) six car set. Close by is the extremely rare ACE E/2 LNWR 4.4.2 Tank. In the background, 'Cheltenham Spa Express' comprising eight Hawksworth and Collett C/12 40 cm coaches  first introduced at Telford Guildex 2005. The magnificent Bassett-Lowke style 'Nunney Castle' was kindly loaned to us for working the train by Mike Little. The ACE Castle will be along in 2006.*

# FOOTNOTE ON COLLECTING

Normally manufacturers would not be concerned with the secondary market for their products, but in view of the many spurious claims concerning 'Limited Editions' with all those silly certificates and subliminal claims of investment potential I thought a few words on the subject might be in order. I am of course only addressing the subject of models and not books and prints or sculptures for whom limited editions might, if issued by honest publishers, be relevant I stress the word *might*.

Gauge 0 trains are not stocks and shares and they are bought for a variety of reasons but I suspect the pure pleasure of ownership and operating ranks high and investment an accidental by product.

So accepting we live in times where every bit of bric-a-brac is offered for appraisal on TV programmes, the internet and the seemingly never ending stream of auctions, I will comment in so far as I think that ACE Trains might form part of the pantheon of 'collectables'in the future.

ACE Trains certainly satisfy some basic criteria as set out below.

• **They have been made in commercial quantities although in some cases very small ones.**

*(The size of the run is determined by the disciplines of production, tooling amortisation, sub-contractors minimum quantitities for components versus what is the probable size of the market. All a manufacturer offering a limited edition does is reverse the equation and starts with the probable market and works backwards to the unit cost. When I see limited editions of 5000 plastic model trains I marvel at the gullibility of all concerned. Of course the eventual numbers will never be known, neither will, the customers who pay full price ever meet the ones who buy the same item at 50% or less of the original price when the limited run becomes even more limited due to lack of sales or the temptation to run on a few more.*

*I have gone on at length on this topic because it should be pointed out that virtually none of the great pre–war and early post-war train manufacturers used this ploy and their products have become true collectables with not a numbered certificate in sight. We try to be in that 'old fashioned' mould, both in our marketing and in our attempt to continue the tradition of the original Hornby, Marklin, Bing and Bassett-Lowke Companies.*

*It is the accident of survival and the magic of the product rather than the artificiality of manufactured rarity that matters in these things).*

• **ACE Trains are principally made of metal. I mention this because of my long held view that plastic will never have the long term appeal of metal when applied to model railway stock.**

• **The provenance of the ACE line is readily available in printed matter supplemented by this book which is a contemporary survey of events by participants rather than a retrospective view (with all its elements of at best intelligent surmise on some topics that have become obscured in the mists of time).**

• **Lastly but by no means least the production of ACE Trains is of a standard that is unlikely to be superceded in the years to come.**

Events since various items have become obsolete indicate that ACE products will achieve modest investment status quicker than many other contemporary items. Remember that when comparing the second hand prices achieved for ACE that a full 17.5% of VAT has been added to the original price.

I will not offer any general suggestions as to which particular ACE items will be most sought after but rakes of C/1 GWR and LMS Clerestory roofed stock might be front runners in the short term. Only Carette offered anything similar and they have become way out of the financial reach of most assuming they can be found in good condition. Finding a specifically factory named A4 (E/4) might also be fun down the years as indeed will apply to the 'Castle Class' due in 2006 when it is planned to offer every name and number the class bore.

## TABLE OF MANUFACTURED ITEMS

## LOCOMOTIVES

### E/1    4-4-4 Tank Engine, 1996-1997 (24 V AC/DC)

ESB/1    SR E492 black gloss or satin *
ESG/1    SR B604 green gloss or satin *
ELM/1    LMS 4-4-4 maroon gloss or satin (several named)
EMB/1    LMS 4-4-4 black gloss or satin
ELG/1    LNER 4-4-4 green satin
ELB/1    LNER 4-4-4 gloss or satin
EGW/1    GWR 7202 green satin
ECR/1    CR 4-4-4 blue gloss or satin
EMR/1    Metropolitan 108 maroon satin
EET/1    ETAT 2-2-2 black satin
EPO/1    PO 2-2-2 grey satin
EPL/1    PLM red satin (a few named)
END/1    Nord brown satin
END/2    Nord green satin
EES/1    EST black satin
EES/2    EST brown satin
ENZ/1    NZR black satin
    * 44 of the E/1 series in Southern livery were given
      factory produced names at the request of customers
      (1996/97)

### E/2    4-4-2 Tank Engine, 1997 (24V DC with isolating switch)

E/2LB    LB&SCR 22 brown gloss
E/2S     Southern 2001 green gloss
E/2LN    L&NWR 40 black gloss
E/2LM    LMS 6822 maroon gloss
E/2BR    BR 32085 black gloss
E/2NZR   NZR green gloss Sp. Edn. (Railmaster Exports NZ)

### E/3    2-6-2 Tank – Postponed

### C/1E    3-Car EMUs, 1999 (24V AC/DC with isolating switch)

C1E/LM   Broad Street - Richmond maroon LMS 3-car unit
C/1      Extra Trailer Car 3/1/3 for this set
C1E/Met  Baker Street – Harrow brown Metropolitan 4-car unit
C1E/S    Southern 3-car unit V & L route boards carried. (Green) *
C/1      Extra Trailer Car for C1/ES 1st.

C/1G     3-car German Triebwagen set
    * White and grey roof versions

### E/4    A4- Pacific – 2002 – 2005 (24V AC/DC twin motors with isolating switch)

**With Valances**
E/4    LNER Apple green
E/4    LNER Silver grey
E/4    LNER pre-war Garter blue
**Without Valances**
E/4    LNER black restricted names (Tender displaying NE)
E/4    LNER post-war Garter blue
E/4    BR 1948 Thompson blue
E/4    BR 60007 'Sir Nigel Gresley' Express blue Special Edition for the A4 Society.
E/4    BR Brunswick green (one named Terence Cuneo)
E/4    BR Brunswick green double chimney

Most names available. Special personal names available in 2002. Apple Green – part of run named after the great Gauge 0 makers. W J Bassett-Lowke, Frank Hornby etc. Early Garter blue versions satin finish with large head lights and bold smokebox lining.

### E/5    Range of British outline 0-6-0 Tender Locos. All 24DC (AC special order) with isolating switch

Q Class  SR Black/ SR Plain Green
        BR  Black
J 19     GER/LNER   Black
        GER Blue
        BR Black
J11      GCR/LNER  GCR Lined Black/LNER Black
        BR Black

J 19     LNER Black
        BR Black

4F       LMS Black/ LMS Plain Maroon
        BR Black

Pickersgill    CR Blue
        LMS Black
        BR Black

| | | |
|---|---|---|
| J36 | NBR Black (WW1 names) | |
| J36 | LNER Black | |
| | BR Black | |

Class 644  GWR Green (Cambrian Green)
         BR Black

C3      LBSCR Brown
        SR Black
        BR Black

**E/6      Ex LNER A3 Pacific (24V DC isolating switch)**

LNER Doncaster Green
LNER Black
BR Blue
BR Brunswick Green
USA 1968 Version.

Restricted names
'Windsor Lad' 'Diamond Jubilee' 'Blink Bonny'
'Grand Parade' 'Papyrus' and ' Flying Scotsman'.

This locomotive will be available with blank name
plates and unnumbered.

# COACHES

**C/1      35cm Non-Corridor Stock, 1999 Tin printed. Some**
         **of the French coaches have clerestory roofs**

| | |
|---|---|
| C/1 | LMS maroon set of 3.* (conversion kits available) |
| C/1 | LNER light teak set of three |
| C/1CL | LNER ex-GER teak clerestory set of 3 |
| C/1 | GWR dark brown + cream ** |
| C/1 | Southern green set of three C/1 |
| C/1 | Metropolitan brown set of 3 |
| C/1 | LBSCR brown + white set of 3 |
| C/1 | Caledonian plum + white set of 3 |
| C/1 | LNWR brown + white set of 3 |
| C/1 | BR maroon set of 3 |
| C/1 | HRCA 30th Anniversary set of 3 |
| C/NZ | NZR as above but with NZ crest set of 3 |
| C/1D | German Triebwagen set of 3 |
| C/1F | Etat green set of 3 |

| | |
|---|---|
| C/1F | Est Multi coloured set of 3 |
| C/1F | PO green set of 3 |
| C/1F | Nord green set of 3 |
| C/1F | SNCF green  set of 3 |
| C/1F | French outline baggage car – green |
| C/1F | The PLM Set comprising five coaches will be intro duced in 2006. The Set will include the Postal, Car, Baggage Car and three Passenger Cars. |

* Clerestory Roof
** All available with Clerestory Roof

**C/2      Merseyside Express Sets** (Silvered windows)

Set A    LMS maroon composite 4195
         LMS maroon all 3rd 4195
         LMS maroon restaurant car 4799
         LMS maroon all 1st 4183
         LMS maroon brake 3rd 26133 – All five above boxed as
         one set.

Set B    LMS maroon composite, no name boards 4195
         LMS maroon all 3rd, no name boards 4195
         LMS maroon brake 3rd, no name boards 26133

**C/3      LMS Stanier Main Line Coach Kits, 2000**

These have lower roofs and cut-out windows. They
come with a choice of the following destination boards:
'The Royal Scot', 'The Merseyside Express',
'The Mancunian' and 'The Yorkshireman'. Apart from
the unpainted roofs all other parts were pre coloured.

**C/4      LNER Gresley Bow Ended Stock, 2003**
(Clear windows)

The coaches are supplied with slots in the roof  coach
roof boards to fit them carrying the name 'Flying Scots
man'. Available either with or with out cut-out windows.
The first batch made of Set A had no internal partitions
but later ones did or you could have them retro-
spectively fitted. Rear working light on the brake end.

**C/4      LNER Bow Ended Gresley Teak Stock, 2003**
(Black Windows)
All C/4s are Gresley Bow Ended Teak Stock The

coaches are supplied with slots in the roof and coach roof boards to fit them carrying the name 'Flying Scots man'. A run of only 50 of each. Rear working light on the break end. Corridor partitions where appropriate.

Set A     Set of three with rear light as standard
Set B     Set of three complementing Set A
             Single Buffet Car and 1st/3rd Comp

**C/5**       **BR Mk.1 Coaches, 2003** (Blood and Custard)

All sets include internal compartments where appro priate. Rear working light on the brake end of Set A. All with punched out windows. Name boards for 'The Elizabethan' included.

Set A     Set of 3
Set B     Set of 3 to complement Set A *
             BR restaurant car (single)
             BR full brake with rear light (single)
             * Also supplied with Corgi/Bassett-Lowke boxed Royal Scot Set.

**C/6**       **LNER 1926 Gresley Articulated Sleeping Car Set**
             Name boards (Kings X – Edinburgh)

**C/7**       **Coronation Articulated Coaches, 2004** (with coach lights and rear light)
blue + white (C) + (B) (all with Silver roofs)
blue + white (A) + (G)
blue + white (D) + (H) Six coaches in boxed set.
The summer car known as The Beaver tail was available as a single unit in 2005.

**C/8**       **1938 Record Breaking Set 2004**

1 x 6 car Coronation Set with ACE /Wright Dynamometer car

**C/9**       **West Riding Limited Set** (with coach lights and rear light)

Similar to C/7 set but with grey roofs

**C/10**      **Tourist Stock 2005** (with coach lights and rear light)
Green and Cream with off white roofs. Two articulated units and two single bogie cars.

**C/11**      **Silver Jubilee Set 2005** (with coach lights and rear lights)
Seven car articulated set including triple unit with kitchen car.

**C/12**      **GWR (40 cm series) 2005**
(all fitted with insulated wheels and unconnected rear lights) All coaches are Hawksworth unless indicated otherwise. PCB Board for light connection fitted to one brake end.

Set A     Brake 3rd/ Corridor Composite/Corridor First Nos 1779/7798/8002
Set B     Brake Composite/Corridor Third/Open Third (Collett) Nos 7381/831/1297
             Singles
             Buffet Car (Collett) No 9676
             Full Brake No 29

**C/13**      **BR Mk 1 2005/6** (in Green/Choc/Cream/Maroon)
(insulated wheels and unconnected rear lights as above)

             Southern region
Set A     Brake Composite /Corridor Second/Corridor First.
Set B     Brake Second/Corridor Composite/Open Second
             Similar Sets A and B for Western Region and Midland Region
             Singles for all regions- Full Brake/Restaurant/Buffet Car/Open First.

**C/14**      **BR Mark 1 Pullmans** 2005 (insulated wheels and unconnected lights as above)

Set A     Kitchen First 'Eagle'/Parlour First 'Amethyst'/Parlour Second No 349
Set B     Kitchen Second No 336/Parlour First 'Emerald'/Hadrian Bar
Set C     Kitchen First 'Falcon'/ Parlour Second No 351/Kitchen Second No 338
             Single Coach Full Brake.

All C/13 and C/14 Coaches fitted with Commonweatlh fully spring bogies.

## ACE/WRIGHT SERIES 2000 ONWARDS

This series set new standards in a small runs of ready-to-run special vehicles. The models include lithographed heavily varnished card applied to ACE C/1/C/4/5 and 6 coaches.
Various Stock issued from 2003 through 2005
GWR full brake with low roof
GWR full brake with clerestory roof
LMS full brake Stanier c1930
SR parcel van c1930 with ribbed roof
LMS ex-MR mail van clerestory
GWR siphon with pre-war lettering
LNER 5219 full brake teak 'The Flying Scotsman'
LMS Stanier Postal van
LNWR Postal Van. SR Cinema Coach
GWR Ocean Mails Coach. LMS Scenery Van.

## WAGONS

**G/1     Petrol/Spirit Tank Wagon, 2004**
These are sold in sets of three and they will have inter changeable couplings. The bodies are lithographed in four colours and are fitted to a detailed chassis with brake gear. The chassis has dropout side frames for lubricating axle boxes.

| | |
|---|---|
| Set 1 | Set of 3 (ACE Trains Oil /Mobiloil/Esso (Yellow) |
| Set 2 | Set of 3 (Esso (Grey)/Wakefield Castrol/Regent |
| Set 3 | Set of 3 (Pratts High Test/Pratts Spirit(Green)/ Similar (Brown) |
| Set 4 | Set of 3 Anglo American Oil/Motor BP Spirit(Yellow)/ Colas (Red) |
| Set 5 | Set of 3  Redline Glico/Shell Motor Spirit/Royal Daylight |
| Set 6 | Set of 3  National Benzole Mixture/Pool(Grey)/Colas (Blue) |
| Set7 | Set of 3 BP British Petrol( Green)/Power Ethyl/BP Motor Spirit (Grey) |
| Set 8 | Set of 3 Mobiloil/Esso (Yellow)/ Pool (Black) |

**G/1M     Milk Tank Wagons, 2004**
These are also sold in sets of three and are the same as the petrol tanks but without cross strapping and riveting. They also have a smaller filler cap with a valve on either side.

| | |
|---|---|
| Set A | United Dairies white  Set of 3 |
| Set B | Express Dairy white Set of 3 |
| Set C | Nestles Milk white Set of 3 |

**G/2     Goods Vans 2006**

A series of 4 wheeled Goods Vans in Grey and Brown in GWR /LMS/SR/LNER and BR with fully detailed chassis.

**G/3     A 4 wheeled open wagon in grey and brown 2006**

## ACCESSORIES  (AC/1 and AC/1A)

The Ace Constructor Series was introduced in April 2002 and the first item is an all-over glazed roof which is 1' high and 2' long and coded AC/1.
A pair of platforms and ramps also available as AC/1A. The Canopy Sets AC/1 sold outside the UK include glass panels those in the USA Perspex..

A terminus building is also planned. The illustration in the book will not necessarily be the final form of this building.

## MISCELLANEOUS

Other boxed accessories include Rear Light Sets/Coach Light Sets/ Pre cut C/1 Seating Sets/Continental bogie sets/British style bogie sets/Motorised bogie sets and Clerestory roof sets for C/1 series. Also packs of coach boards, LMS, BR, GWR trains.

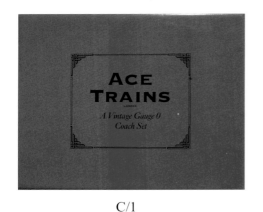

C/1

C/11

C/1 Clerestory

E/4

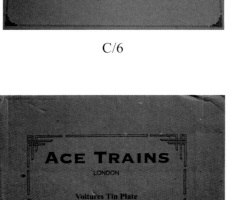

C/1 Singles

C/1/E (three coaches)

C/6

C/2 (five coaches)

C/12 Singles

Note: C/3 (LMS Kit) had a plain brown box without lettering

C/1F

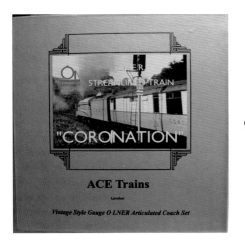

C/7

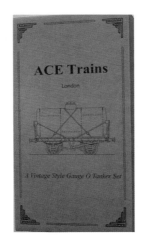

G/1 – G/1M

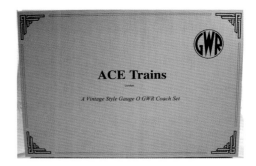

C/12

C/1E/2 Singles

E/1/2

C/4/5

C/4/5

C/10

C/9

ACE/Wright

C/8

# A4 (E/4) Ace Issues – 2003-2005

## LNER - Garter Blue (with Valances)
1st series with thicker screened lining on smoke box and large headlights.
Velvet finish.
2nd series decal applied smokebox lining. Small headlights. Gloss finish.
Silver Fox
Silver Link
Great Snipe
Mallard
Kingfisher
Kestrel
Dominion of Canada
Empire of India
Commonwealth of Australia
Osprey
Golden Fleece
Golden Shuttle
Golden Plover
Sir Nigel Gresley
Capercaillie
Gargency
Pochard
Terence Cuneo
Fred Saxton
Golden Eagle (available through Weaver models in USA – non standard blue)
**Silver Jubilee Locos**
Silver Link
Quicksilver
Silver King
Silver Fox

## LNER - Apple Green (with blackened side plates)
Golden Eagle
Kingfisher
Falcon
Kestrel
Sea Eagle
Woodcock
Osprey
Great Snipe
Sparrow Hawk
Merlin
Wild Swan
Frank Hornby
W J Bassett-Lowke
Stanley Beeson

R F Stedman
WHG Mills
Gebr. Bing
George Carette
Gebr. Marklin
Joshua Lionel Cowan
Count Giansanti Coluzzi
Marcel Darphin
Henry Greenly
Allen Levy
Andries Grabowsky
This great gauge 0 makers series were numbered 7143 onwards.

## Wartime Black (without valances marked NE on tender)
Sir Ralph Wedgwood
Mallard
Sir Charles Newton
Andrew K McCosh
Peregine
Sir Nigel Gresley

## LNER - Garter Blue (without valances)
Lord Farringdon (with British Railways in full lettering style)
Silver Fox
Silver Link
Sir Ralph Wedgwood
Mallard
Kingfisher
Kestrel
Merlin
Union of South Africa
Empire of India
Seagull
Dwight D Eisenhower
Sir Nigel Gresley
Commonwealth of Australia
Woodcock

## BR - 'Thompson Blue' 1949
Kingfisher
Merlin
Sea Eagle
Woodock

## BR - Blue 1950/51
Guillemot
Gannet
Sir Nigel Gresley (for A4 Society)
Mallard

Union of South Africa
Dominion of New Zealand

## BR - Brunswick Green (all with double chimneys) later series with blackened side plates.
Andrew K McCosh
Sir Nigel Gresley
Dwight D Eisenhower
Union of South Africa
Dominion of Canada
Empire of India
Commonwealth of Australia
Dominion of New Zealand
Silver King
Silver Fox
Sparrow hawk
Bittern
Mallard
Kingfisher
Falcon
Miles Beevor
Woodcock
Golden Plover
Seagull
Note: All pre 1939 style locos issued with valances. Post 1940 issued without valances. Double Chimneys fitted to Mallard, Capercaillie, Seagull, Peregine, Terence Cuneo all apple green locos bearing numbers 7143 onwards and all BR Green locos.

## 2006 onwards E/4/2
**2-rail version of selected locos**
**LNER – Garter Blue (with or without valances)**
Mallard
Silver Fox
Sir Nigel Gresley
Wartime Black
Peregine
BR - Green
Dwight D Eisenhower
Mallard
Sir Nigel Gresley

## E/4/S
**A live steam high pressure version is in preparation.**
**LNER - Garter Blue (with valances)**
Mallard
Sir Nigel Gresley

# Index

**A**

A1s  17
A3s  17
A4s  17, 72, 76, 116
A4 (E5)  113
AC/1 Canopy kit  64
ACE/Wright Series  80
Alchem Trains  17, 37, 72
Andries Grabowsky  12, 17, 19, 20, 23, 36, 40, 62, 66, 69, 72, 73, 76, 80, 81, 96, 97, 98, 102, 104
Antique Toy Collectors Club of America  32
AS  17, 20, 21, 33, 63
Aster  20, 30, 105
A Century of Model Trains  11, 17

**B**

Bangkok  52, 69, 72, 76, 80, 88, 96, 113, 122
Bassett-Lowke  12, 20, 61
Bing  20
Blood and Custard  72, 88, 116
Book of Trains  66
British Railways  21
Budd, Ron  20
Burnett tin toy kits  69

**C**

C/1  41, 48, 54, 61, 62, 66, 70, 71, 72, 75, 80, 81, 92, 126, 127, 128, 129
C/10  54, 69, 87, 116, 128
C/11  41, 62, 80, 88, 128
C/1E  66, 126
C/1F  62, 88, 127
C/2  61, 62, 66, 69, 80, 127
C/3 kits  69
C/4  61, 72, 80, 88, 113, 122, 127, 128
C/4 Gresley Teak  80
C/5  72, 88, 108, 113, 116, 118, 128
C/7  92, 100, 128
Canopy  64, 76, 99, 129
Carette  20
Chad Valley  9, 62
Charlotte Levy  48, 72
CIWL  20
Classic Toy Trains  42, 112
Clive Lamming  25
Corgi  9, 18, 19, 80, 87, 88
Coronation Coaches  76
Count Giansanti  20

**D**

Darstaed  12, 20, 72, 81
Dave Cole  30
Dave Moss  80

Dudley Dimmock  12

**E**

E/1  11, 17, 21, 24, 26, 27, 28, 33, 34, 36, 42, 45, 47, 53, 58, 69, 75, 80, 96, 126
E/2  21, 22, 24, 25, 37, 47, 53, 121, 126
E/3  113
E/4  61, 72, 76, 98, 126
E/5  20, 86, 95, 97, 106, 109, 126
Edward Exley  19, 67
Elettren  20, 98
Emily  101
EMU  43, 56, 62, 66, 109
Est  20, 62, 63, 127
ETS  66

**F**

First World War  62
Fortnum and Mason  76, 95, 97
Frank Hornby  12
FS Pacific  20
Fulgurex  20

**G**

G/1M Milk Tanker sets  88
G/1 Tanker series  88
Gauge 0 Guild  48
Gauge 1  20
GGolden Eagle  76
Great Western  18
GWR Castle Class  88

**H**

HO  12, 21
Hornby  20, 21, 25, 38, 41, 47, 52, 61
Hornby Dublo  11, 62, 76, 116
Hornby Railway Collectors Association  11, 21
HRCA Journal  24, 38, 43, 44, 82

**I**

Ian Lanes  67
Ian Layne  62
India  20, 40, 62, 66, 69, 70, 72, 76
Ives  20

**J**

Jep  20, 63
John Agnew  100
John Beadsmore  21
John Cooper  36, 62, 80
John Kitchen  21, 49, 88
John Mayo  29, 80
John Ovendon  80, 94
John Pentney  41
John Shawe  76, 97

**K**

Kings Cross 17

**L**

L&NWR 21, 126
LB&SCR 21, 126
Leicester 18, 88, 110
Len Mills 9, 19, 23, 80, 88, 97, 120
Lima 18, 61
Lionel 20
LMS 19, 21, 40, 42, 66, 69, 88, 118, 126, 127, 129
LNER 30, 62, 69, 72, 88, 100, 126, 127, 129
London Toy and Model Museum 12, 17, 31, 102
Louis Hertz 20
Luffs printing works 54

**M**

Madras 52, 62, 66, 72
Maldon Rail Centre 88
Mallard 76, 92
Marcel Darphin 12, 81
Marklin 20, 22, 45
Mark 1 Pullmans 81, 88, 128
Martin Wright 80
Meccano 11, 25, 80
Merseyside Express 61, 66, 127
Metropolitan 41, 52, 62, 66, 72, 126
Mettoy 9, 62
Michelle Grabowsky 40, 72, 96
Mike Allen 60, 80, 91
Muhlkreis Junction 80, 88, 99

**N**

N2s 17
Narisa Chakrabongse 12
New Cavendish Books 3, 6, 11, 12, 18, 62, 80, 91, 119
Nolfa 62
Nord 62, 63, 66, 81, 92, 126, 127
Northampton 12, 18
NZR 21, 22, 126

**P**

Peter Hauer 45
Petrol Tanker 68
PLM 20, 33, 66, 88, 126, 127
PLM E/1 33
PO 62, 126, 127
Princess Elizabeth 66

**Q**

Quentin Lucas 67

**R**

Railmaster Exports 53, 126
Riding the Tinplate Rails 20

Ron Budd 20
Ron McCrindell 32
Ron Wheele 30
Roy Fearn 62

**S**

Silver Jubilee 88, 116, 128
Sir Nigel Gresley 76, 89, 92, 126
SNCF 62
Southern 17, 21, 34, 66, 70, 75, 86, 88, 126, 127, 128
Southern EMU 66
Stanley Beeson 19
St Mawes Bay 17
Suba Brothers 66
Switzerland 12, 80

**T**

Taipei 28, 40, 69, 70
Taiwan 20
Tambaram 51
Terence Cuneo 107, 126
Terry Barnicote 80
Thailand 37, 66, 72, 76
The ACE Electric Train Company Ltd 37, 72
The Bassett-Lowke Story 12
The Vintage Toy Train Co. Ltd 37
Tinplate 20, 22, 25, 61
Tourist Stock 54, 69, 87, 128
Train Collectors Society 88
Triebwagens 62
Tuttlingen 33, 73, 81, 86, 92, 96, 97, 98, 102

**U**

Uhlenbroch 21, 24, 66

**V**

Van Rymsdyk 17
Vic Hunt 18
Vijay Velappan Kumar 72
Vintage Toy Trains Company 72
Volta 17, 36

**W**

Warship' diesel 88
Weaver Incorporated 76
Wilag 20
World War II. 18
Wright 66, 78, 80, 96, 128

**Z**

Zug 12, 19

*The Old and the New*

Top: What Trish Arnold bought her husband Elsdon (at left) for Christmas at the Rotorura 2005 Show in New Zealand – the last LNER blue 'Dominion of New Zealand' with a Coronation Set, here seen on acceptance trials. Half way around the world at Telford the next ACE main line Loco will be the Great Western Castle. Mike Little's fabulous short run example reflects fairly accurately the upcoming batch produced ACE offering.